Quick Fix

Quick Fix

Sudden Fiction

Ana María Shua

Translated and Introduced by
Rhonda Dahl Buchanan

Illustrations by
Luci Mistratov

WHITE PINE PRESS / BUFFALO, NEW YORK

White Pine Press
P.O. Box 236, Buffalo, New York 14201
www.whitepine.org

Pieces in this book appeared in Spanish in the following books:
La sueñera. Buenos Aires: Minotauro, 1984. Buenos Aires: Alfaguara, 1996. Emecé,
2006. *Casa de geishas*. Buenos Aires: Sudamericana, 1992. *Botánica del caos*. Buenos
Aires: Sudamericana, 2000. *Temporada de fantasmas*. Madrid: Páginas de Espuma,
2004.

Some of the translations in this collection have appeared previously in the fol-
lowing publications, and have been revised for this book: *American Voice; The Café
Irreal: International Imagination; Confluencia; Literal: Latin American Voices; Miriam's
Daughters: Jewish Latin American Women Poets* (Ed. Marjorie Agosín. Santa Fe:
Sherman Asher Publishers); and *Words Without Borders: The Online Magazine for
International Literature*.

Publication of this book was made possible, in part, with funds from the
University of Louisville and by grants from the National Endowment for the
Arts, which believes that a great nation deserves great art and with public funds
from the New York State Council on the Arts, a State Agency.

Cover art: Luci Mistratov

Printed and bound in the United States of America

ISBN 978-1-893996-91-5

Library of Congress Control Number: 2007943939

for my husband and personal chef Bob Buchanan

—R.D.B.

Contents

Introduction by Rhonda Dahl Buchanan - 13

I. from *La sueñera* ◐ *Dream Catcher*

I - 21
4 - 22
6 - 23
9 - 24
12 - 25
16 - 26
19 - 27
25 - 28
27 - 29
31 - 31
47 - 32
56 - 33
60 - 34
77 - 35
85 - 36
89 - 37
92 - 39
100 - 40
114 - 42
116 - 43
135 - 44
170 - 45
171 - 47
176 - 48
179 - 49
204 - 50
205 - 51
213 - 51

214 - 53
215 - 54
223 - 56
231 - 58
235 - 59
250 - 60

II. from *Casa de geishas* ℗ *Geisha House*

El reclutamiento /Recruitment - 62
Simulacro / Simulacrum - 63
En el patio /On the Patio - 64
Caricia perfecta / Sublime Caress - 65
Mirones / Voyeurs - 66
Ataduras / Bondage - 67
Sádicos / Sadists - 68
Abaratando costos / Cutting Costs - 69
Sofisticación / Sophistication - 70
Los pulcros son así / Neat Freaks - 71
La Que No Está / The Girl Who Is Not Here - 72
Las mujeres se pintan / The Painted Ladies - 73
Tatuaje / Tatoo - 74
La Insaciable / Miss Insatiable - 75
Para todos los gustos / To Each His Own - 76
Para princesa muy lectora / For the Literate Princess - 77
Doncella y unicornio I / Maiden and Unicorn I - 79
Doncella y unicornio V / Maiden and Unicorn V - 81
Ermitaño II / Hermit II - 82
Cenicienta I / Cinderella I - 83
Cenicienta II / Cinderella II - 84
Los enanos son mineros /The Dwarves are Miners - 85

Golem y rabino I / Golem and Rabbi I - 87
Golem y rabino III / Golem and Rabbi III - 88
Golem y rabino IV / Golem and Rabbi IV - 89
Golem y rabino V / Golem and Rabbi V - 91
El héroe a tiempo / In the Nick of Time - 93
Sapo y princesa I / The Princess and the Frog I - 94
Sapo y princesa II / The Princess and the Frog II - 95
Dudosa prueba / Insufficient Proof - 96
Pista falsa / Dead End Clue - 97
¡Huyamos! / Run for Your Lives! - 98
Espíritu / Heart and Soul - 98
El vasto número / The Vast Number - 99
El viejo y la muerte / The Old Man and Death - 100
Terreno /Grave Plot - 102
Los amantes / The Lovers - 104
Cuatro paredes / Four Walls - 105
El respeto por los géneros /Respect for Genres - 106
Caníbales y exploradores /Cannibals and Explorers - 107
La temporada de fantasmas / Ghost Season - 108
Taller literario I / Literary Workshop I - 109
Teóloga / Theologian - 110
Robinson deafortunado / Unfortunate Robinson - 112
Zafarrancho de naufragio / Abandon Ship! - 113
El autor y el lector / The Author and the Reader - 114

III. from *Botánica del caos* (☯ *Botany of Chaos*

Amores entre guardián y casuarina /
        Romance between Guard and Magnolia - 119
Cuidado con las mujeres / Beware of Women - 121
Abuela no nos cree / Grandma Doesn't Believe Us - 122

El padre y el hijo / Father and Son - 124

Si viajar en el tiempo fuera posible / Time Travel - 125

El Día del Juicio Final / Judgment Day - 126

Después de Caín / After Cain - 127

El Dios Viejo del Fuego / The Ancient God of Fire - 130

Información útil / Pertinent Information - 133

Los auxilios de la medicina / Medical Assistance - 134

Profetas y cataclismos IV / Prophets and Catastrophes IV - 135

Profetas y cataclismos VI / Prophets and Catastrophes VI - 136

Alí Babá / Ali Baba - 137

En el avión / On the Plane - 141

Por falta de pruebas / Lack of Proof - 142

Con alivio / What a Relief - 143

La más absoluta certeza / Most Absolute Certainty - 144

Lo que pudo ser /What Could Have Been - 145

Ese gato / That Cat - 146

Tabú cultural / Cultural Taboo - 148

Desnudez /Nudity - 149

Mago que cree en su magia /
The Magician Who Believes in Magic - 150

El insuperable arte de Ma Liang /
The Unsurpassable Art of Ma Liang - 151

Malos consejos / Bad Advice - 152

Excesos de pasión / Excesses of Passion - 153

Hombre sobre la alfombra /Man on the Rug - 154

Vuelo de libertad / Flight of Freedom - 155

Próceres en el pizarrón /
Founding Fathers on the Blackboard - 156

IV. from *Temporada de fantasmas* (☯ *Ghost Season*

Temporada de fantasmas / Ghost Season - 159
Concatenación / Concatenation - 160
Su viuda y su voz / His Widow and his Voice - 161
El niño terco / The Stubborn Boy - 162
La ardilla verosímil / The Trusty Squirrel - 165
El pájaro azul / The Blue Bird of Happiness - 166
Hombre que huye / Man on the Run - 167
Los corredores / Runners - 168
Una confesión / A Confession - 169
La persecución / The Hunt - 170
El Murciélago / The Bat - 171
La profesional / The Professional - 173
Creación I: la construcción del universo /
        Creation I: The Making of the Universe - 175
Una prueba de fe / Test of Faith - 176
Mirando enfermedades / Contemplating Diseases - 177
Interrogatorio clínico / Medical Diagnosis - 179
En la silla de ruedas / In the Wheelchair - 181
La desmemoria / Forgetfulness - 182
La caída del mundo / On Shaky Ground - 183
Por única vez / One Time Only - 184
Casa prestada / Borrowed House - 185
La ciudad soñada / Dream City - 186
Sueños de niños / Children's Dreams - 187
Convivencia imposible / Impossible to Live With - 189
Van Gogh II / Van Gogh II - 190
Motín a bordo / Mutiny on Board - 191
La hora de las gaviotas / Seagull Time - 193
El que no tuvo infancia / The Man without a Childhood - 194
Poetas / Poets - 195

Alimentos del mar / Seafood - 196
Formicario / Formicary - 199
About the Author - 201
About the Translator - 202
About the Artist - 203

INTRODUCTION

Rhonda Dahl Buchanan

In this age of speed and technology, when people are distracted by email, BlackBerries, and iPods, the short short story has definite appeal for those addicted to reading who can barely find time to open a book. Even the ancient Greeks understood the relationship between speed and fiction. As Italo Calvino tells us in his essay on the virtues of "Quickness" in literature, the god of communication and the inventor of writing is none other than Mercury, the agile deity of winged feet (*Six Memos for the Next Millenium*). The short short story, referred to as sudden fiction, microfictions, and blasters in English, and *cuentos brevísimos* and *ficciones relámpagos* (lightning fiction) in Spanish, shares many of the virtues of poetry. In fact, Julio Cortázar, one of the Argentine masters of this literary genre, refers to the short short story as *el hermano de la poesía*, or poetry's brother. Sudden fiction presents a challenge to the author, for like poetry, it requires exactness, control, virtuosity, and no small amount of courage. If the traditional short story wins over the reader by a knockout after a series of blows, as Cortázar proposes in *La casilla de Morelli*, in mini-fiction the knockout must come in one decisive punch. As Irving Howe observes in the introduction to *Short Shorts: An Anthology of the Shortest Stories:* "Everything depends on intensity, on one sweeping blow of perception. In the short short the writer gets no second chance."

Of all Latin American countries, Argentina boasts the greatest number of writers who have cultivated this rebellious literary genre: masters such as Jorge Luis Borges, Adolfo Bioy Casares, Julio Cortázar, Marco Denevi, Enrique Anderson Imbert, Raúl Brasca, and Luisa Valenzuela; however, without a doubt, Ana María Shua is the reigning queen of short shorts, with four volumes of *cuentos brevísimos* published to date, and the promise of more to come. The recipe for Shua's success in the art of miniature fiction consists of her ingenious blending of precise language, incisive humor, and incredible imagination, resulting in a unique style and execution of these little brain teasers, some as short as seven words. Proof of her success is the fact that new editions of all four of her original books of sudden fiction are in the process of being published, beginning with the first, *La sueñera,* which was released in Buenos Aires in 2006 by Editorial Emecé.

Like the short short story, which resists classification and definition, Ana María Shua has confounded the critics who have attempted to label her fiction. Born in Buenos Aires in 1951, the author began her literary career at the tender age of fifteen, when she published an award-winning volume of poetry, *El sol y yo (The Sun and I).* Although Shua has published over fifty books in nearly every literary genre, including novels, short stories for adults and children, sudden fiction, humorous books of Jewish folklore, essays, and screen plays, the author has admitted in interviews that the short short story is her favorite genre, perhaps because it enables her to showcase her trademark talents: an innate capacity for synthesis and conciseness, and the use of humor and irony to reflect upon the human condition. Indeed, her books of short short stories are my favorites as well.

I first met Ana María Shua in Buenos Aires in 1992, the year her second book of sudden fiction, *Casa de geishas,* was published. In fact, this was the very first book the author gave me personally, a gift that would mark the beginning of a long friendship and a productive professional relationship, but our "history" actually dates back to 1981, the year that the author sent me her first novel *Soy paciente (Patient,* 1980) and her first volume of short stories *Los días de la pesca (Fishing Days,* 1981), while I was still a graduate student at the University of Colorado in Boulder. I learned that after having me as a student in her class on contemporary Argentine literature, the writer Beatriz Guido, who spent one year as a Visiting Professor at CU during the dictatorship, suggested to Shua that she send me her books. After finally meeting the author a decade later, I began writing critical articles about her short short stories and novels, and publishing translations of her sudden fiction in journals, online magazines, and anthologies. In 2001, I edited a volume of twenty-six critical essays entitled *El río de los sueños: Aproximaciones críticas a la obra de Ana María Shua,* which includes five articles about her sudden fiction. About the time that her fourth book of short short stories, *Temporada de fantasmas (Ghost Season)* was published in 2004, I approached Shua with the idea of publishing a bilingual illustrated anthology that would include a selection from all four of her books of short short stories. Everything came together in the spring of 2006 when Dennis Maloney, editor/publisher of White Pine Press, agreed to publish the manuscript in The Secret Weavers Series, and I befriended Luci Mistratov, a talented Russian artist and illustrator of books who had recently settled in Louisville. I shared each translated story with Luci, sometimes resorting to theatrical techniques to explain the ironic twists and implicit humor of certain stories, and together we decided which ones would lend themselves well to an illustration. The result is a collection of delightful whimsical drawings that capture the essence of Shua's incisive humor.

The stories in this book may be read at random or according to the order in which the original books were published. In fact, it is the perfect book to carry with you for those moments when you must wait for an appointment, a flight, your turn at the check-out line, or if you find yourself stuck in traffic. Shua's first book of sudden fiction, *La sueñera (Dream Catcher)*, is a collection of 250 untitled stories, first published in Buenos Aires in 1984, and most recently in 2006. As the title implies, the unifying themes of this volume are dreams, nightmares, sleep, or the lack thereof. This book should come with a warning label cautioning that reading (or translating) too many of these stories may lead to insomnia. My personal favorite of her four books, *Casa de geishas (Geisha House)*, first published in 1992, is a collection of 215 stories divided into three sections. In the first, which lends its name to the title of the book, Shua employs sarcasm and irony to explore one of the oldest professions on Earth, prostitution. These little "quickies," or what I like to call in Spanish *"textículos,"* explore the nature of desire and are metaphors for the literary process itself. Just as there is a book to please every reader, there is a geisha to satisfy every erotic fantasy; however, before entering Madame Shua's house of pleasure and perversions, the clientele should be warned that nothing is as it seems. In the section of the book entitled "Versions," the reader may recognize the characters of traditional fairytales, myths, and legends whose stories have been subverted with an unexpected ending. I have taught Shua's *brevísimos* in my language and literature classes, and students love them, particularly the ones I refer to as "fractured fairytales," which offer revisions of such beloved childhood tales as Cinderella, Snow White and the Seven Dwarfs, and The Princess and the Frog. In her third book *Botánica del caos (Botany of Chaos)*, published in 2000, Shua plays with a number of diverse topics regarding the bizarre nature of mankind and the universe, including myths of the Genesis and the Final Judgment Day. The blasters or minifictions selected from the fourth book, *Temporada de fantasmas (Ghost Season)*, published in 2004, run the gamut from the mysteries of human relationships to the capricious whims of the gods, with something in between to please every reader.

There is nothing more ludicrous than a long introduction to a book of short short stories, but before closing, I would like to express my gratitude to those who made this book possible. First and foremost, I would like to thank Ana María Shua for collaborating with me and clarifying any doubts that I had about the meaning of the stories. I would also like to thank David William Foster, who published translations of thirteen of the *Geisha House* stories in the *Rocky Mountain Review of Language and Literature,* and graciously gave me permission to publish my own "versions" of those tales. I cannot thank Luci Mistratov enough for the ingenious line drawings that accompany the stories and the spectacular illustration that adorns the cover. I dedicate this book, with much love and appreciation, to my husband Bob Buchanan, who prepared so many scrumptious meals while I translated these stories, and then read each one of them after dinner and offered suggestions that improved them. What more can a translator ask for? Perhaps an editor to make my dream of publishing a bilingual anthology of Ana María Shua's sudden fiction a reality, and for that I am eternally grateful to Dennis Maloney and Elaine LaMattina of White Pine Press. I would also like to acknowledge the generous contribution that the University of Louisville made toward the publication of the illustrations in this book.

Those who are addicted to reading know that oftentimes it is impossible to put a book down once you open it. Ana María Shua is certainly aware of this danger, and once remarked about her book *Casa de geishas* that it was her intention to set a more subtle trap for her readers, one that would entice them to return to the pages of her book time and time again, at the risk of becoming entangled forever in her web of intrigue. This collection of Ana María Shua's sudden fiction offers the reader a daily "quick fix," measured in 139 safe doses, or a complete overdose, if consumed in one sitting. I hope you enjoy your trip!

I. from

La sueñera ℗ *Dream Catcher*

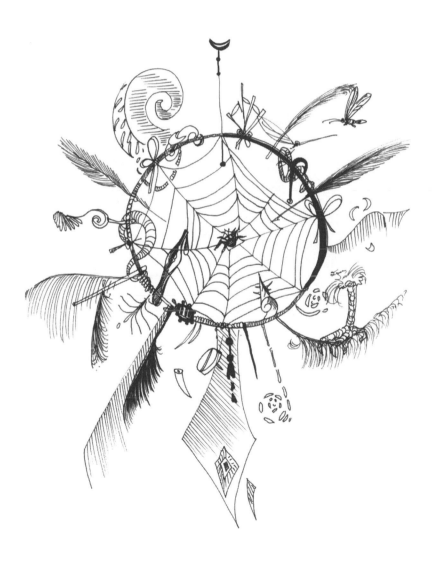

I

Para poder dormirme, cuento ovejitas. Las ocho primeras saltan ordenadamente por encima del cerco. Las dos siguientes se atropellan, dándose topetazos. La número once salta más alto de lo debido y baja suavemente, planeando. A continuación saltan cinco vacas, dos de ellas voladoras. Las sigue un ciervo y después otro. Detrás de los ciervos viene corriendo un lobo. Por un momento la cuenta vuelve a regularizarse: un ciervo, un lobo, un ciervo, un lobo. Una desgracia: el lobo número treinta y dos me descubre por el olfato. Inicio rápidamente la cuenta regresiva. Cuando llegue a uno, ¿logrará despertarme la última oveja?

I

To fall asleep, I count sheep. The first eight jump over the fence one after the other. The next two collide, banging heads. Number eleven jumps higher than it should and glides down for a smooth landing. Then five cows jump, two of them flying. A deer follows them and then another. A wolf comes running after the deer. For a while, the count settles down: a deer, a wolf, a deer, a wolf. Then disaster strikes: wolf number thirty-two sniffs me out. Quickly I begin counting backwards. When I get to number one, will the last sheep manage to wake me up?

4

Quiero dormir. Ante los Dioses del Sueño, postrada, imploro. Éste es tu sueño, me responden furiosos. Entonces, quiero despertar. Caminarás, me ordenan, por un largo pasillo. Hallarás dos puertas. Una de ellas guarda tu despertar. La otra, la más monótona de las pesadillas, que es la muerte. Debes abrir una: el azar o tu ingenio pueden favorecerte. Camino por un largo pasillo hasta alejarme de los Dioses del Sueño. Veo dos puertas. Junto a ellas, inmóvil, espero. Creado por Dioses tan poderosos como los del sueño, tarde o temprano sonará el despertador.

4

I want to sleep. Kneeling before the Gods of Slumber, I plead. This is your dream, they respond in a huff. All right then, I want to wake up. You will walk, they command me, down a long corridor. You will find two doors. Behind one lies your awakening, behind the other the most boring nightmare of all, death. You must open one: your fate depends on chance or your judgment. I walk down a long corridor, away from the Gods of Slumber. I see two doors. I wait next to them, without budging. Created by Gods as powerful as those of slumber, sooner or later the alarm clock will go off.

6

En la selva del insomnio no es necesario internarse. Crece a mi alrededor. No hay bestias más feroces que los grillos. En un claro, creo divisar el sueño. Me acerco lentamente, acallando, para no despertarlo, el rumor de mis pasos. Sin embargo, cuando recojo la red, está vacía. Para volver a encontrar la pista tengo muchos recursos: enumerar los árboles del bosque, olvidarlos, concentrarme en el curso de las aguas de un río, tomar café con leche (varias tazas), recordar hacia atrás o hacia adelante. Entretanto, por un momento, me distraigo, y el sueño se arroja sobre mí. Me duermo tan feliz que no recuerdo ya quién era el cazador y quién la presa.

6

There's no need to venture into the jungle of insomnia. It grows all around me. There are no beasts more ferocious than crickets. In a clearing, I believe I spot sleep. I approach slowly, quietly, so my footsteps don't awaken it. But when I gather the net, it's empty. I have a few tricks to find its trail again: number the trees of the forest, ignore them, focus on the river current, drink lattés (several cups), recollect going backward or forward. In the meantime, I get distracted for a moment and sleep ambushes me. I fall asleep so overjoyed that I no longer remember who was the hunter and who the prey.

9

Fumando, me quedo dormida. Del otro lado, soy feliz: es un buen sueño. El cigarrillo cae sobre la alfombra y la enciende. La alfombra enciende la cortina. La cortina enciende la colcha. La colcha enciende las sábanas. De la casa queda sólo un montón de cenizas. Del otro lado, sigo siendo feliz: ya nada puede obligarme a despertar.

9

I fall fast asleep while smoking. On the other side, I'm happy: it's a good dream. The cigarette falls on the rug, setting it on fire. The rug ignites the curtain. The curtain ignites the mattress, the mattress the sheets. All that's left of the house is a pile of ashes. On the other side, I'm still happy: now nothing can make me wake up.

12

¿De qué materia están hechos los sueños? Desconozco los suyos, caballero. Los míos están hechos de queso Gruyere y son muy ricos, un poquito picantes. Eso sí: con los agujeros hay que tener cuidado.

12

What stuff are dreams made of? I'm not familiar with yours, sir. Mine are made of Gruyere cheese and are very delicious, just a little sharp. One thing for sure, you have to watch out for the holes.

16

En la oscuridad confundo un montón de ropa sobre una silla con un animal informe que se apresta a devorarme. Cuando prendo la luz, me tranquilizo, pero ya estoy desvelada. Lamentablemente, ni siquiera puedo leer. Con la camisa celeste clavándome los dientes en el cuello me resulta imposible concentrarme.

16

In the darkness, a pile of clothes on a chair appears to be a shapeless animal about to devour me. After I turn on the light, I calm down, but now I'm awake, and unfortunately I can't even read. With that light blue shirt sinking its teeth into my neck, I find it impossible to concentrate.

19

En la oscuridad, un montón de ropa sobre una silla puede parecer, por ejemplo, un pequeño dinosaurio en celo. Imagínese, entonces, por deducción y analogía, lo que puede parecer en la oscuridad el pequeño dinosaurio en celo que duerme en mi habitación.

19

In the darkness, a pile of clothes on a chair can appear to be, for example, a small dinosaur in heat. So just imagine, by deduction and analogy, what the small dinosaur in heat that sleeps in my room might appear to be in the darkness.

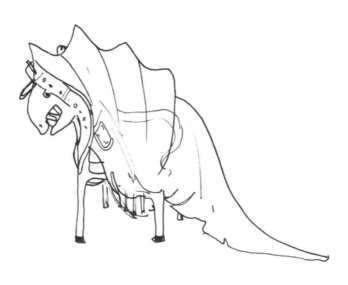

25

Mi papá no está contento conmigo. Me mira más triste que enojado porque sabe que le oculto un secreto. Estás muerto, quisiera decirle. Pero tengo miedo de que no venga más.

25

My dad's not happy with me. He looks at me, more sad than angry, because he knows I'm keeping a secret from him. You're dead, I'd like to tell him, but I'm afraid he won't come back.

27

Desde el hueco de un árbol, me llama un caballero. Sálveme, señorita, me ruega. Hace ya varios siglos que me encuentro encantado, esperando a la doncella que venga a liberarme. Yo no soy señorita, maleducado, soy señora, le contesto ofendida. (Un caballero de varios siglos es demasiado viejo para mí.)

27

From a hollow in a tree, a gentleman calls out to me. Save me, Miss, he begs me. I've been bewitched for many centuries, just waiting for a maiden to come and rescue me. I'm no maiden, you brute, I'm a lady, I answer offended. (A man who's been around for centuries is too old for me.)

31

Abro la canilla pero el agua se niega a salir. Para llamarla, los sioux proponen cierta danza que reproduzco sin resultados. Acercando un fósforo encendido, intento atraerla. Una gota bien dirigida lo apaga: del chorro, ni noticias. Como la portera no sabe nada y en Obras Sanitarias me atiendan mal, decido ir a las fuentes. Apenas me acerco a la orilla, el Río de la Plata se retira, amontonándose en la costa uruguaya. Yo al plomero no lo llamo: por un problema así, me va a cobrar un ojo de la cara.

31

I turn on the faucet but the water refuses to come out. To invoke it, the Sioux recommend a dance, which I perform with no results. I attempt to lure it by placing a lit match under the faucet. A well-aimed drop snuffs it out, leaving no sign of a trickle. Since the landlady is clueless and the Water Company doesn't give me the time of day, I decide to go to the source. Just as I approach the shore, the River Plate recedes, swelling on the Uruguayan coast. Forget it, I'm not going to call a plumber. For a problem this big, he'll charge me an arm and a leg.

47

Cuidado, señora, me dice mi analista. Nos aproximamos a la zona de los rápidos. Acostada boca arriba en el diván, se me llenan las orejas de lágrimas. Algunas piedras emergen en la correntada. Pasito a pasito intentamos el cruce. En la mitad, pierdo pie. Para no caerme, me aferro a la peluca de la doctora, que se me queda en las manos. Veo a mi analista, con su propio pelo pegado al cráneo, hundiéndose en la catarata de mi angustia. Y, doctora, le grito desde la orilla, ¿para qué le sirven ahora sus honorarios?

47

Be careful, madam, my shrink tells me. We're approaching the rapids. Lying face up on the couch, my ears fill up with tears. A few rocks emerge in the rushing current. Step by step we try to get across. Halfway there, I slip. To avoid falling, I cling to my doctor's wig, which I'm left holding in my hands. I see my shrink, with her real hair plastered to her skull, drowning in the falls of my anguish. Tell me, Doctor, I scream to her from the shoreline: What good will your fees do you now?

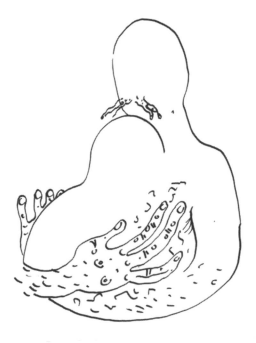

56

A veces me despierto de visiones horribles, agitada, angustiada,
llorando. Para calmarme le pido a mi marido que me deje apoyar
la cabeza en su cuerpo y me abrace bien fuerte con todos sus
tentáculos.

56

Some times I wake up from horrible visions, restless, upset,
and crying. To calm down, I ask my husband to let me lay my
head on his body, and to embrace me tightly with all his
tentacles.

60

Apenas me despierto, mi ropa se apresura a colgarse de las perchas. El espejo se abraza a la pared como si nunca la hubiese abandonado y el velador vuelve a la mesita de luz con el paso cansado de un noctámbulo a la hora del desayuno. Cuando abro los ojos, todos están más o menos en su lugar. La cómoda, para disimular, silba un tango bajito. Si no fuera por el desorden de mi ropero, podría creer que aquí no ha pasado nada.

60

As soon as I wake up, my clothes rush to hang themselves up. The mirror clings to the wall as if it had never abandoned it, and the night stand returns to the bedside, dragging its tired feet like a sleep-walker at breakfast time. When I open my eyes, everything is where it belongs, more or less. The dresser, to cover up, whistles a tango softly. If it weren't for the chaos in my closet, I might believe nothing's been going on here.

77

De los vegetales de hojas perennes, ninguno se reproduce tan rápidamente como mi biblioteca. Sus vástagos, sus brotes y retoños amenazan con asfixiarme en primavera.

77

Of all the species with perennial leaves, none reproduces more quickly than my library. In springtime, its shoots, buds, and sprouts threaten to smother me.

85

El verdadero valor de los cuentos de Sherezada no residía en su atractivo sino, por el contrario, en su hipnótica monotonía. Gracias a sus aburridísimas historias fue la única entre las múltiples esposas del sultán que logró hacerlo dormir todas las noches. Protegido de las torturas del insomnio, el sultán recompensó a Sherezada con el mejor de los premios: su propia vida. Los cuentos que componen la colección que se conoce como *Las mil y una noches*—y que, en verdad, no carecen totalmente de interés—fueron creados muchos años después por la bella Dunyasad, hermana menor de la sultana, para entretener a sus reales sobrinos.

85

The real value of Scheherazade's tales did not rest on their intrigue, but rather just the opposite, on their hypnotic monotony. Thanks to her extremely boring stories, she was the only one of the sultan's many wives who succeeded in making him fall asleep each night. Sheltered from the tortures of insomnia, the sultan rewarded Scheherazade with the greatest of all prizes: her own life. The stories of that collection, which is known as *The Arabian Nights*, and which, truth be told, are not totally lacking in interest, were created many years later by the sultan's little sister, the beautiful Dunyazad, to entertain her royal nieces and nephews.

89

¿Qué le hubiera gustado ser si no fuera lo que es?, le pregunta el periodista a la vampiresa. Me hubiera encantado tener sangre de periodista, contesta ella, más interesada en su yugular que en su micrófono.

89

What would you have liked to have been if you weren't what you are? the journalist asks the vampiress. I would have loved to have partaken of the blood of a journalist, she replies, much more interested in his jugular than his microphone.

92

Un hombre sueña que ama a una mujer. La mujer huye. El hombre envía en su persecución los perros de su deseo. La mujer cruza un puente sobre un río, atraviesa un muro, se eleva sobre una montaña. Los perros atraviesan el río a nada, saltan el muro y al pie de la montaña se detienen jadeando. El hombre sabe, en su sueño, que jamás en su sueño podrá alcanzarla. Cuando despierta, la mujer está a su lado y el hombre descubre, decepcionado, que ya es suya.

92

A man dreams that he loves a woman. The woman runs away. The man sends the dogs of his desire after her. The woman crosses a bridge over a river, climbs a wall, leaps over a mountain. The dogs swim across the river, jump the wall, and come to a halt at the foot of the mountain, panting. Still dreaming, the man knows that never in his wildest dream will he ever catch her. When he awakens, the woman's at his side, and the man realizes, disappointed, that she's already his.

100

Mientras Aladino duerme, su mujer frota dulcemente su lámpara maravillosa. En esas condiciones, ¿qué genio podría resistirse?

100

While Aladdin sleeps, his wife tenderly rubs his magic lamp. Under such conditions, what genie could resist?

114

Son frecuentes—casi un tópico literario—las situaciones en que uno o más personajes enjuician a su autor acusándolo de homicidio, de insensibilidad, de mutilaciones físicas o espirituales. En cambio, sólo una excesiva vanidad hace que ciertos autores se quejen de los vergonzosos extremos a los que han sido arrastrados por sus propios personajes.

114

They're so common, almost a literary theme, those situations in which one or more characters judge their author, accusing him of homicide, callousness, even physical or spiritual mutilations. On the other hand, only excessive vanity leads certain authors to complain about the embarrassing extremes they've been forced to endure at the hands of their own characters.

116

Con un correctísimo conjuro invoco a Satanás. Sin embargo, debo resignarme a conversar con su secretario. Mi señor es ubicuo y omnisciente, anuncia con solemnidad. Pero me entrega una solicitud para llenar por triplicado. Decididamente la burocracia es un infierno.

116

With an infallible incantation I invoke Satan. Nevertheless, I must resign myself to speak with his secretary. My lord is omnipresent and omniscient, he announces solemnly as he hands me a form to fill out in triplicate. Most definitely bureaucracy is hell.

135

Peor, mucho peor que perderse (y tan sedientos) en el desierto de una página en blanco: caer desprevenidos en el hondo pozo oasis de una o.

135

Worse, much worse than getting lost (and so thirsty) in the desert of a blank page, is falling, without warning, into the deep oasis well of an "o."

170

En el mundo hay un señor que es Dios sin saberlo. Su poder,
sin embargo, no es absoluto. Sus deseos, sus fantasías, sus más
vagas intenciones se realizan de un modo que parece arbitrario
por estar sujeto a leyes desconocidas, aunque naturales. Sus secre-
ciones estomacales provocan, por ejemplo, ríos de lava en algún
lugar de la tierra. Su mal humor desencadena guerras. Procesos
más sutiles que tienen lugar en cada una de sus células o sus
cabellos rigen la vida privada de los hombres. Ese señor no es
inmortal. Cuando muera es posible que sus poderes sean trans-
feridos a otros por nacer. También es posible que el mundo desa-
parezca por completo, pero eso no lo sabremos nunca.

170

There exists in the world a man who is God, although he
doesn't realize it. His power, nevertheless, is not supreme. His
desires, his fantasies, his most abstract intentions are carried out
in a seemingly random manner that is subject to mysterious,
albeit natural laws. For example, his gastric secretions provoke
rivers of lava somewhere on the planet and his bad moods
unleash wars. More tenuous processes, which take place in each
of his cells or hair follicles, govern the private lives of mankind.
That man is not immortal. When he dies, his powers may be
transferred to someone about to be born. It's also possible that
the world may disappear altogether, but that's something we'll
never know.

171

Mi hija usa la misma palabra para llamar a los pies, a los pájaros y a los ombligos. Esto es un pie, hija mía, y no un pájaro, la corrijo con severidad, tomando entre mis manos uno de sus piececitos tibios, palpitantes, alados y cubiertos de plumas.

171

My daughter uses the same word for feet, birds, and belly buttons. This is a foot, baby, not a bird, I correct her adamantly, while holding in my hands one of her warm, throbbing little winged feet, covered with feathers.

176

Durante cien años durmió la Bella. Un año tardó en des-perezarse tras el beso apasionado de su príncipe. Dos años le llevó vestirse y cinco el desayuno. Todo lo había soportado sin quejas su real esposo hasta el momento terrible en que, después de los catorce años del almuerzo, llegó la hora de la siesta.

176

Sleeping Beauty slept for one hundred years. She took one year to stretch after her prince's passionate kiss. She took two years to get dressed and five to eat breakfast. Her royal husband put up with all this without complaining until that dreaded moment when, after fourteen years of lunch, it was time for a nap.

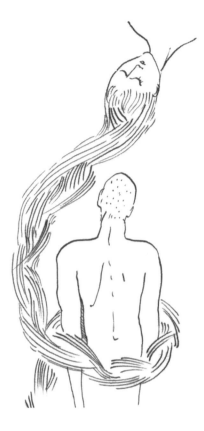

179

Mientras dormía, Dalila le ha cortado el pelo y, sin embargo, Sansón se despierta aliviado a una realidad más benigna que su atroz pesadilla, la calvicie.

179

While he was sleeping, Dalilah cut his hair, and yet, Samson awakens with relief to a reality more benign than his terrible nightmare: baldness.

204

Lo malo del alcohol es que se me sube enseguida. Y continúa subiendo sin encontrar freno ni tope hasta que yo misma comienzo a preguntarme dónde, pero dónde, dios mío, estará mi cabeza.

204

The bad thing about alcohol is it goes straight to my head, and finding nothing to stop it, keeps going until I myself begin to wonder, oh God, where, oh where can my head be?

205

Le cuento a un amigo un sueño en el que él interviene. Vas a tener que explicarme el final, me dice, como si los sueños lo tuvieran, como si pudiera estar segura de que ha terminado.

205

I tell a friend about a dream I had with him in it. You'll have to explain the ending to me, he says, as if dreams had endings, as if I could be certain it's over.

213

Toda bruja tiene su escoba o la desea.

213

Every witch has her broom or longs for one.

214

Lo cierto es que las sirenas desafinan. Es posible tolerar el monótono chirrido de una de ellas, pero cuando cantan a coro el efecto es tan desagradable que los hombres se arrojan al agua para perecer ahogados con tal de no tener que soportar esa horrible discordancia. Esto les sucede, sobre todo, a los amantes de la buena música.

214

One thing's for sure, mermaids can't keep a tune. It's possible to tolerate the monotonous screeching of one of them, but when they sing together, the sound is so awful that men hurl themselves into the sea to perish by drowning rather than endure that horrible discordance. This happens, especially, to lovers of fine music.

215

Compra esta lámpara: puedo realizar todos los deseos de mi amo, dice secretamente el genio al asombrado cliente del negocio de antigüedades, que se apresura a obedecerlo sin saber que el genio ya tiene amo (el dueño del negocio) y un deseo que cumplir (incrementar la venta de lámparas).

215

Buy this lamp: I can fulfill my master's every wish, the genie whispers to the astonished customer in the antique shop, who hastens to obey him without realizing that the genie already has a master (the owner of the shop) and a wish to fulfill (increase the sale of lamps).

223

Para dormir cómoda, me despojo de todo lo superfluo. Sentada en el borde de la cama me quito lentamente la ropa. Dejo caer los brazos, que se estiran sobre la alfombra como gruesas serpientes. Con un movimiento brusco me desprendo de las piernas y sacudiendo la cabeza hago volar mis facciones (ojos, boca, nariz) por todos los rincones de la habitación. Y continúo, hasta que no queda entre las sábanas más que mi sexo, que de todas maneras nunca duerme.

223

To sleep comfortably, I rid myself of everything superfluous. Sitting on the edge of the bed, I slowly take off my clothes. I drop my arms, which stretch out on the carpet like thick serpents. With a quick jerk, my legs come off, and shaking my head, my features (eyes, mouth, nose) go flying to the far corners of the room. And I continue until the only thing left between the sheets is my sex, which never sleeps anyway.

231

Qué hermoso despertar con el canto de los pájaros, oír en la mañana soleada sus gorjeos que crecen en intensidad y alegría mientras el sol trepa hacia su cenit y siguen aumentando de volumen por la tarde hasta que parece el mundo entero, ya en el crepúsculo, una caja de resonancia para sus dulces trinos que se hacen cada vez más y más fuertes cuando empieza la noche y descubrimos que nunca, nunca vamos a poder dormir si no se callan (y no se callan) esos malditos pájaros.

231

How lovely to wake up to birds singing, to listen on a sunny morning to their chirping, which increases in volume and cheerfulness as the sun rises toward its zenith, and gets louder in the afternoon until at dusk it seems as if the entire world were a music box resounding with their sweet songs, which become louder and louder as night falls and we realize that we'll never, never ever get to sleep if those damn birds don't shut up (and they don't).

235

Entre las formas del suicidio: retroceder en el tiempo hasta el momento de su propia concepción, impedirla.

235

Among the forms of suicide: go back in time to the moment of your own conception and prevent it.

250

La flecha disparada por la ballesta precisa de Guillermo Tell parte en dos la manzana que está a punto de caer sobre la cabeza de Newton. Eva toma una mitad y le ofrece la otra a su consorte para regocijo de la serpiente. Es así como nunca llega a formularse la ley de gravedad.

250

The arrow shot from the accurate crossbow of William Tell splits in half the apple that is about to fall on Newton's head. Eve takes one half and offers the other to her partner, to the delight of the serpent. This is how the law of gravity never came to be formulated.

II. from
Casa de geishas ℗ *Geisha House*

El reclutamiento

Las primeras mujeres se reclutan aparentemente al azar. Sin embargo, una vez reunidas, se observa una cierta configuración en el conjunto, una organización que, enfatizada, podría convertirse en un estilo. Ahora la madama busca a las mujeres que faltan y que ya no son cualquiera sino únicamente las que encajan en los espacios que las otras delimitan, y a esta altura ya es posible distinguir qué tipo de burdel se está gestando y hasta qué tipo de clientela podría atraer. Como un libro de cuentos o de poemas, a veces incluso una novela.

Recruitment

The first women appear to be recruited at random, but once assembled, a certain configuration may be detected within the group, an organization that, if accentuated, could develop its own style. Now Madam searches for the women she needs, and not just any will do, but only those who fill in the gaps delineated by the others. By now it's possible to discern what kind of brothel is in the works, and even what type of clientele it might attract. Like a book of stories or poems, perhaps even a novel.

SIMULACRO

Claro que no es una verdadera Casa y las geishas no son exactamente japonesas; en épocas de crisis se las ve sin kimono trabajando en el puerto y si no se llaman Jade o Flor de Loto, tampoco Mónica o Vanessa son sus nombres verdaderos. A qué escandalizarse entonces de que ni siquiera sean mujeres las que en la supuesta Casa simulan el placer y a veces el amor (pero por más dinero), mientras cumplan con las reglamentaciones sanitarias. A qué escandalizarse de que ni siquiera sean travestis, mientras paguen regularmente sus impuestos, de que ni siquiera tengan ombligo mientras a los clientes no les incomode esa ausencia un poco brutal en sus vientres tan lisos, tan inhumanamente lisos.

SIMULACRUM

Of course it's not a real House and the geishas aren't exactly Japanese; when times are tough they can be seen working the docks without kimonos, and if they don't go by Jade or Lotus Flower, neither are Monica or Vanessa their real names. So why be shocked that in the so-called House those who feign pleasure and sometimes love (but for more money) may not even be women, as long as they comply with health regulations. Why be shocked that they may not even be transvestites, as long as they pay their taxes, or that they may not even have navels, as long as their clients aren't bothered by that somewhat cruel absence on their smooth bellies, so inhumanly smooth.

En el patio

En verano se baila en el patio, con faroles y lepidópteros nocturnos. La danza es lenta, las parejas se abrazan, los cuerpos se buscan y se unen, se adhieren los vientres y los pechos, la música es densa, el aire es viscoso, para despegarlos basta con sumergirlos un ratito en agua tibia.

On the patio

In summertime, they dance on the patio, with lanterns and nocturnal moths. Slow dancing, the partners embrace, bodies seeking bodies, interlocking, bellies clinging to bellies and chests to chests. The music is heavy, the air thick. All it takes to separate them is a quick dip in lukewarm water.

Caricia perfecta

No hay caricia más perfecta que el leve roce de una mano de ocho dedos, afirman aquellos que en lugar de elegir a una mujer, optan por entrar solos y desnudos al Cuarto de las Arañas.

Sublime Caress

No caress is more sublime than the slight brush of a hand with eight fingers, declare those who, instead of choosing a woman, opt to enter alone and naked into the Room of the Spiders.

MIRONES

A los mirones se les hace creer que miran sin ser vistos. Se les dice que la pared transparente junto a la que se ubican simula ser, del otro lado, un espejo. En realidad, sólo un vidrio corriente los separa de los felices exhibicionistas. En estas combinaciones se destaca la madama, hábil en reducir costos.

VOYEURS

The voyeurs are led to believe they watch without being seen. They're told the transparent wall in front of them appears, on the other side, to be a mirror. Actually, just a pane of glass separates them from the jubilant exhibitionists. Madam, adept at cutting costs, excels at these combinations.

Ataduras

Muchos prefieren que se los ate y la calidad de las ataduras varía, como es natural, de acuerdo con el peculio de la gozosa víctima: desde lazos de seda hasta lazos de sangre. Y es que en el fondo nada ata tanto como la responsabilidad de una familia (ciertamente el más caro de los placeres-sufrimientos).

Bondage

Many prefer to be bound, and naturally, the kind of bondage varies depending on the resources of the aroused victim: from silk ties to blood ties. After all, when you get down to it, nothing binds more than family responsibility—certainly the most expensive of all painful pleasures.

SÁDICOS

Para aquellos que se complacen en el sufrimiento o en la humillación del prójimo, se propone una combinación de estímulos placenteros de los que no se excluyen ciertos programas de televisión.

SADISTS

For those who take pleasure in the suffering or humiliation of others, a combination of gratifying stimulations are recommended, of which certain TV shows are not excluded.

Abaratando costos

Algunos masoquistas disfrutan con la idea de que otros asistan a su humillación. Los que pueden hacerlo contratan dos o más pupilas. Pero para los verdaderamente ricos está prevista la participación de cinco mil extras y el alquiler del estadio. (Se rumorea que los espectadores son sádicos, que se les cobra la entrada.)

Cutting Costs

Some masochists relish the thought that others witness their humiliation. Those who have the means hire two or more girls. But for the filthy rich, a stadium may be rented with five thousand extras. (It's rumored the spectators are sadists who are charged admission.)

Sofisticación

Para los más sofisticados (pero admitamos que se trata de una perversión muy cara), la madama está en condiciones de contratar los servicios de su propia esposa.

Sophistication

For the most sophisticated (but let's admit it's a very expensive perversion), Madam is willing to provide the client with the services of his own wife.

Los pulcros son así

Los pulcros usan muchas prendas de vestir y se las quitan lentamente. Al cabo del primer año se han sacado ya el sombrero y los calcetines, que acomodan con parsimonia sobre una silla. Cuando por fin están desnudos, miran a su pareja con cierta decepción y algunos exigen que se la cambien por una mujer más joven. Como todos los demás, pagan por hora.

Neat Freaks

Neat freaks wear many articles of clothing and take them off slowly. By the end of the first year, they've finally removed their hats and socks and placed them carefully on a chair. When naked at last, they look at their partner with some disappointment and a few demand she be exchanged for a younger woman. Like all the rest, they pay by the hour.

La Que No Está

Ninguna tiene tanto éxito como La Que No Está. Aunque todavía es joven, muchos años de práctica consciente la han perfeccionado en el sutilísmo arte de la ausencia. Los que preguntan por ella terminan por conformarse con otra cualquiera, a la que toman distraídos, tratando de imaginar que tienen entre sus brazos a la mejor, a la única, a La Que No Está.

The Girl Who Is Not Here

None is more successful than The Girl Who Is Not Here. Although still young, many years of dedicated practice have allowed her to perfect the very subtle art of absence. Those who request her end up settling for another, whom they possess with indifference, trying to imagine that they hold in their arms the best, the only, The Girl Who Is Not Here.

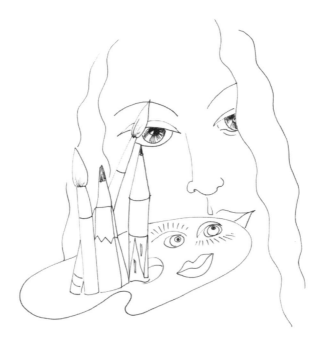

Las mujeres se pintan

Las mujeres se pintan antes de la noche. Se pintan los ojos, la nariz, los brazos, el hueco poplíteo, los dedos de los pies. Se pintan con maquillajes importados, con témperas, con lápices de fibra. En el alba, ya no están. A lo largo de la noche y de los hombres, se van borrando.

The Painted Ladies

The ladies paint themselves before night falls. They paint their eyes, nose, arms, toes, and the crease behind their knees. They paint themselves with imported makeup, acrylics, with pencils and brushes. By dawn, they have vanished. With each passing hour and each man, they fade away.

Tatuaje

En cierto recóndito paraje de su anatomía, Jezabel ha soportado un complejo tatuaje. Muchos han pagado por verlo. Los que, gracias a su habilidad o a su fortuna, pueden contarlo, dicen que el dibujo representa un mapa teñido de colores suaves (esa combinación de las tintas con el tono natural de la piel). En el mapa está señalado el punto en el que se encuentra el observador y la ruta que lo llevará a la salida.

Tattoo

On a secret part of her anatomy, Jezabel bears an intricate tattoo that many have paid to see. Those who can describe it, thanks to their dexterity or good fortune, claim the design represents a map tinged with subtle colors, a combination of ink with natural skin tone. The map indicates the location of the observer and the route that will lead him to the exit.

La insaciable

A otra mujer la llaman La Insaciable, como si alguien, alguna vez, saciara algún deseo.

Miss Insatiable

Another woman is called Miss Insatiable, as if a desire could ever be fulfilled.

Para todos los gustos

Para los vampiros golosos, mujeres gordas, lánguidas, diabéticas, con cuello de Modigliani. Para vampiros francamente perversos, bestialistas, juguetonas jirafas. Para vampiros que se complacen en su propio sufrimiento, ciertas botellas de vidrio, importadas de Italia (en las que el vino ha sido reemplazado), cuyos cuellos estallan al ser mordidos con gozoso dolor.

To Each His Own

For sweet-toothed vampires: fat, listless, diabetic women with Modigliani necks. For extremely perverse vampires into bestiality: jesting giraffes. For vampires who luxuriate in their own suffering: imported Italian glass bottles whose wine has been replaced and whose necks burst when bitten with rapturous pain.

Para princesa muy lectora

A tal punto están previstos todos los deseos y provisto todo lo necesario para satisfacerlos, que se incluye entre el personal a un sapo bien alimentado para princesas que deseen experimentar ciertos trucos o intentar mutaciones. Después de veinte princesas se lo reemplaza por uno recién salido del estanque. De acuerdo con el resultado de las experiencias, al anterior se lo entierra o se le rinde pleitesía.

For the Literate Princess

All possible desires are anticipated and everything needed to satisfy them is provided to the extent that even a well-fed frog is included among the personnel for princesses who wish to experiment with certain tricks or attempt transformations. After twenty princesses, the frog is replaced with one fresh out of the pond. Depending on the results of the experiments, its predecessor is either buried or paid homage.

Doncella y unicornio I

Hay quienes suponen agotado el tema del unicornio y la doncella por extinción de ambas especies. Sin embargo el diario de hoy publica la fotografía de un caballo con un manchón sanguinolento sobre la frente. El animal asegura haber sido, hasta pocas horas antes de la toma, una auténtica doncella.

Maiden and Unicorn I

Some believe there's nothing more to be said about unicorns and maidens, given the extinction of both species. Yet a photo of a horse with a huge bloody stain on its forehead was published in today's paper. The animal claims to have been, up until a few hours before the picture was taken, an authentic maiden.

Doncella y unicornio V

Es falso que los unicornios acostumbren formar manadas. Tampoco lo hacen las doncellas. Es falso que reúnan en locos aquelarres en los que doncellas desnudas cabalgarían unicornios. Ni las doncellas tienen interés en cabalgar ni a los unicornios les gusta ser montados. Lo contrario, en cambio, a veces es posible. Sobre todo considerando que, si bien los unicornios no tienen inconvenientes en conservar su condición indefinidamente, ninguna anciana doncella se jactaría de haber conservado tan largamente su honra.

Maiden and Unicorn V

It's not true that unicorns usually run in herds, nor do maidens. It's not true that they gather in wild nocturnal covens with naked maidens mounting unicorns. Neither the maidens have any interest in mounting nor do unicorns like being mounted. On the other hand, the opposite is sometimes possible, especially considering that even if unicorns don't mind keeping their horns intact indefinitely, no old maid would brag about having preserved her honor for so long.

Ermitaño II

El ermitaño recibe por correo un grueso volumen. Es un completísimo catálogo de tentaciones. Como cualquiera que aspire a la santidad, el ermitaño es ambicioso y soberbio y decide encargarlas todas. Una flotilla de camiones descarga las tentaciones en las inmediaciones de la eremita. El desierto se transforma en ciudad. El hombre consigue resistir todas las tentaciones pero, en cambio, ya no es ermitaño. Las tentaciones le hacen compañía, lo entretienen, lo distraen de su soledad.

Hermit II

A hermit receives a thick book in the mail, a catalogue offering every possible temptation. Like anyone who aspires to sainthood, the hermit is ambitious and haughty, so he decides to order everything. A fleet of trucks delivers the temptations to a place nearby. The desert becomes a city. The man resists all temptations, but now he's no longer a hermit. The temptations entertain him and keep him company, distracting him from his solitude.

Cenicienta I

A las doce en punto pierde en la escalinata del palacio su zapatito de cristal. Pasa la noche en inquieta duermevela y retoma por la mañana sus fatigosos quehaceres mientras espera a los enviados reales. (Príncipe fetichista, espera vana.)

Cinderella I

At the stroke of midnight she loses her glass slipper on the palace stairs. She tosses and turns all night long and in the morning returns to her exhausting chores while awaiting the royal entourage. (Prince with shoe fetish, wishful thinking.)

Cenicienta II

Desde la buena fortuna de aquella Cenicienta, después de cada fiesta la servidumbre se agota en las escalinatas barriendo una atroz cantidad de calzado femenino, y ni siquiera dos del mismo par para poder aprovecharlos.

Cinderella II

Ever since that Cinderella's lucky break, after each ball the servants wear themselves out on the stairs sweeping a ridiculous assortment of women's shoes, but never a matching pair to walk away with.

Los enanos son mineros

La Reina mala logró su propósito, pero así, dormida, todavía la tienen con ellos. El Príncipe Azul, en cambio, se la quiere llevar. Los enanos se resisten. Blancanieves propone emplearlos como jardineros en el parque que rodea el palacio. Parece una solución sensata.

Pero los enanos no son jardineros sino mineros. Las malezas invaden el parque, los macizos de flores languidecen, las especies más delicadas no sobreviven, el invernadero es un depósito de cadáveres vegetales. Los enanos, mientras tanto, han cavado un túnel que los lleva directamente a la bóveda del Banco Central. Ejerciendo su natural oficio, extraen los lingotes de oro que respalda la emisión monetaria del reino. El subsiguiente caos económico provoca la caída de la familia reinante. Encabezan la sublevación los verdaderos jardineros, despedidos por causa de los enanos.

Blancanieves y el Príncipe se refugian en la casita del bosque. La Reina mala está vieja y aburrida y de vez en cuando los visita: su hijastra es ahora una mujer de cierta edad y el espejo mágico le dice que las hay más bellas. (El espejo es malvado pero no miente.) Los enanos se separaron y escriben desde países lejanos y diversos.

El Príncipe se acuerda a veces de su primera esposa y se pregunta cómo habría sido su vida si no se hubiera separado de Cenicienta.

The Dwarves are Miners

The wicked Queen got her wish, but Snow White, still fast asleep, remains with the dwarves. When Prince Charming comes along and tries to take her away, the dwarves protest. Snow White suggests hiring them as gardeners for the park surrounding the palace, a seemingly practical solution.

But the dwarves are miners, not gardeners. Weeds invade the park, the flowerbeds languish, the most delicate varieties perish, and the greenhouse is a compost pile of organic cadavers. Meanwhile, the dwarves have dug a tunnel that leads them straight to the Central Bank vault. Putting their expertise to good use, they extract the gold ingots that back the kingdom's liquid assets. Economic chaos ensues causing the demise of the reigning family. Heading the uprising are the real gardeners who lost their jobs to the dwarves.

Snow White and the Prince take refuge in the cottage in the woods. The wicked Queen is old and bored and visits them from time to time: her stepdaughter is now a woman of a certain age and the magic mirror tells her that there are others more beautiful. (The mirror is evil but does not lie.) The dwarves have gone their separate ways and write from different far away countries.

The Prince sometimes thinks about his first wife and wonders how his life would have been had he not left Cinderella.

Golem y rabino I

Muchos cabalistas fueron capaces de crear un Golem, pero no todos lograron que su Golem les obedeciera. Se cuenta la historia de un Golem rebelde a quien cierto rabino modeló a su propia imagen y semejanza y que, aprovechando el notable parecido de sus rasgos, tomó el lugar de su Creador. Esta verídica historia es absolutamente desconocida porque nadie notó la diferencia, excepto la feliz esposa del rabino, que optó por no comentarlo.

Golem and Rabbi I

Many kabbalists were capable of making a Golem, but not all could make their Golem obey them. The story is told of a rebellious Golem, shaped by a certain rabbi in his own image and likeness, who exploiting their remarkable resemblance, took the place of his Creator. This true story is completely unknown because no one could tell the difference, except for the rabbi's happy wife, who chose not to comment.

Golem y rabino III

¿Quién somete? ¿Y quién es sometido? Dícese que en cierta ocasión (esta historia sucedió, con variantes, muchas veces) el que se rebeló no fue el Golem sino su Amo. Te prohíbo que me obedezcas, gritó con voz terrible. Y el Golem se vio forzado a realizar la más difícil de las tareas: ser amo de sí mismo. En cambio su Creador, liberado al fin, se dedicó entonces a obedecer puntualmente las órdenes de su suegra.

Golem and Rabbi III

Who subdues and who is subdued? Legend has it that on a certain occasion (this story has taken place many times, with variations) the one who rebelled was not the Golem but his Master. I forbid you to obey me, he shouted in an intimidating voice, thus forcing the Golem to carry out the most difficult task of all: to be his own master. On the other hand, his Creator, now free at last, devoted himself to obeying his mother-in-law's orders.

Golem y rabino IV

¡No me obedezcas!—ordenó su Amo al perplejo Golem que, ansioso por cumplir su orden, la desobedeció al instante, mostrándose aun más servil que de costumbre.

Golem and Rabbi IV

Don't obey me!, the Master ordered the perplexed Golem who, anxious to fulfill his command, disobeyed it immediately, proving himself to be more subservient than ever.

Golem y rabino V

Se toma un trozo de arcilla, se la moldea dándole la forma de un ser humano, se realizan ciertos ritos, se pronuncian ciertas fórmulas, se sopla en la boca de la estatua el aliento vital y la estatua no se mueve ni le crecen las uñas o el cabello, se verifica en el Libro el pasaje correspondiente en busca de algún error, pero cuando se intenta repetir el ritual, el Hombre de Barro ha desaparecido. Se toma otro trozo de arcilla, se la moldea, veintisiete Golems fugitivos, veintisiete errores acechan en las sombras, repiten a coro los salmos para confundir al rabino, qué difícil inscribir así en la arcilla blanda, oh señor ayúdame, la fórmula cromosómica completa.

Golem and Rabbi V

He takes a piece of clay and molds it, shaping it into a human being. He performs certain rituals and utters certain phrases. He blows the breath of life into the statue's mouth, but it doesn't move nor does it grow fingernails or hair, so he checks the appropriate passage in the Book, searching for an error, but when he tries to repeat the ritual, the Man of Clay has vanished. So he takes another piece of clay and molds it: twenty-seven fugitive Golems, twenty-seven errors lurk in the shadows repeating psalms in unison to confuse the rabbi. Oh God help me, under these conditions, it's so hard to inscribe on soft clay the complete genetic code.

El héroe a tiempo

Un monstruo desalmado exige al reino el tributo de sus doncellas, a las que devora. Su apetito de mujeres es cada vez mayor. Ahora se las come sin siquiera constatar su doncellez. Se le imponen al pueblo más sacrificios. El héroe llega a tiempo, corta las tres cabezas de la serpiente y salva a las víctimas. Después, con periódica puntualidad, exige su premio. Se aguarda con esperanza el pronto arribo de otro héroe.

In the Nick of Time

A heartless monster demands from the kingdom a tribute of maidens, and then devours them. His appetite for women grows steadily. Now he eats them without even verifying their virginity. More sacrifices are imposed on the village. The hero arrives in the nick of time, severs the three heads of the serpent, and rescues the victims. Afterwards, with periodic punctuality, he demands his reward. The people anxiously await the imminent arrival of another hero.

Sapo y princesa I

Si una princesa besa a un sapo y el sapo no se transforma en príncipe, no nos apresuremos a descartar al sapo. Los príncipes encantados son raros, pero tampoco abundan las auténticas princesas.

The Princess and the Frog I

If a princess kisses a frog and the frog doesn't turn into a prince, let's not be so quick to blame the frog. Enchanted princes are rare, but for that matter real princesses are also hard to find.

Sapo y Princesa II

Ahora que conocemos el desarrollo de la historia, nos resulta fácil afirmar, admonitoriamente, que la excesiva princesa debió contentarse con el primer milagro. Pero, habiéndose transformado el sapo en un apuesto príncipe, cómo refrenar su natural impulso de besar al príncipe, que se convirtió nueva y definitivamente en sapo.

The Princess and the Frog II

Now that we know how the tale unravels, it's easy for us to declare, admonishingly, that the excessive princess should have been satisfied with the first miracle. But, having transformed the frog into a dashing prince, how could she control her natural impulse to kiss the prince, who turned once again and forevermore into a frog.

Dudosa Prueba

a Samuel Coleridge

Si un hombre desciende en sueños al infierno y se le entrega como prueba un diabólico tridente y al despertar el tridente no está allí, ¿es esa suficiente prueba de que ha logrado salir del infierno?

Insufficient Proof

to Samuel Coleridge

If a man could pass thro' Hell in a dream, and have a devil's pitchfork presented to him as a pledge, and not find that pitchfork in his hand when he awoke, is that sufficient proof he has managed to escape Hell?

Pista falsa

Seguir el reguero de manchas, ¿no será peligroso? ¿Cómo saber que conducen hasta el cadáver, y no hasta el asesino? (Pero las manchas son de tinta y llevan hasta la palabra *fin.*)

Dead End Clue

Couldn't it be dangerous to follow the trail of stains? How can we be sure they lead to the corpse, and not the murderer? (But the stains are ink blots guiding us to the word *end.*)

The End

¡Huyamos!

¡Huyamos, los cazadores de letras est´n aqu´!

Run for Your Lives!

Run, the letter hunters ar_ h_re!

Espíritu

En estas humildes palabras está encerrado todo el espíritu de su autora: "Socorro, socorro, sáquenme de aquí".

Heart and Soul

Captured in these simple words are the heart and soul of their author: "Help, help, get us out of here!"

El vasto número

3452, 3453, 3454 . . . Cuenta, para dormirse, el vasto número de los hombres (los imagina saltando una tranquera) que nunca fueron sus amantes.

The Vast Number

3452, 3453, 3454 . . . To fall asleep she counts (imagining them jumping a fence), the vast number of men who never were her lovers.

El viejo y la muerte

El hombre muy viejo se jactaba de conocer a la muerte porque estaba más cerca de ella que otros hombres. Muchos le preguntaban cómo es, y para cada uno pensaba la respuesta que lo dejaría satisfecho. Es como antes de haber nacido, es como un rinoceronte ciego, es como la cocina de la casa de tu abuela. Así decía, y por sus palabras era amado. Sin embargo, la muerte lo había visitado ya, sin que él fuera capaz de reconocerla: y hacía mucho que estaba en ella sin saberlo.

The Old Man and Death

A very old man bragged about knowing death because he was so much closer to her than others. Many asked him to describe death, and he'd invent an answer that would leave each one satisfied: it's like being in the womb, it's like a blind rhinoceros, it's like your grandma's kitchen. He'd say things like that and was revered for his words. Nevertheless, death had already paid him a visit and, unbeknownst to him, they've been together for a long time.

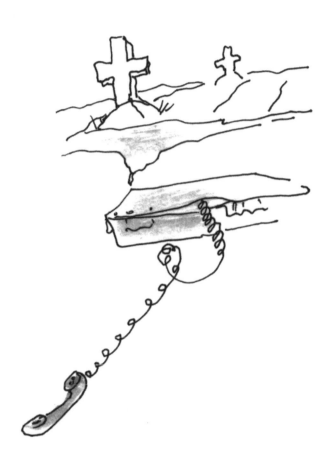

Terreno

Una mujer me llama por teléfono para ofrecerme un terreno en un cementerio privado. Mis excusas no la desalientan: su trabajo consiste en rebatirlas. Con energía y convicción de buena vendedora me fuerza a situarme tan vívidamente en el después de mí que mis colores se deslíen, me trasluzco, se adelgaza mi voz en el teléfono y, lo que es peor para ella, mi firma no tiene ya validez en ningún banco.

Grave Plot

A woman calls to offer me a plot in a private cemetery. My excuses don't discourage her because it's her job to refute them. With the energy and passion of a dedicated saleswoman, she forces me to place myself so vividly in my own afterlife that my color fades, I become translucent, my voice shrinks over the phone and, what's worse for her, my signature's no longer valid at any bank.

Los amantes

Hablaban siempre de una reencarnación que les permitiría besarse en público. Murieron juntos en un accidente, en una de sus citas clandestinas. Él reencarnó en un elefante de circo y ella en una petunia. Como la vida de las petunias es muy breve, se produjo un fuerte desfasaje. En la siguiente reencarnación, los dos fueron humanos, pero con sesenta y tres años de diferencia. Ella llegó a ser Papa y él una graciosa niña a la que se le permitió besar su anillo en una audiencia.

The Lovers

They always dreamed of a reincarnation that would allow them to kiss in public. They died together in an accident during one of their secret rendevous. He came back as a circus elephant and she as a petunia. Since the lifespan of petunias is very brief, this put them out of sync. In the next reincarnation they were both human, but with sixty-three years between them. She became Pope and he an adorable little girl who was granted permission to kiss his ring in an audience.

Cuatro paredes

Siempre encerrada entre estas cuatro paredes, inventándome mundos para no pensar en la rutina, en esta vida plana, unidimensional, limitada por el fatal rectángulo de la hoja.

Four Walls

Forever confined within these four walls, I invent worlds to escape the routine of this flat, one-dimensional life, restricted by the fatal rectangle of the page.

El respeto por los géneros

Un hombre despierta junto a una mujer a la que no reconoce. En una historia policial esta situación podría ser efecto del alcohol, de la droga, o de un golpe en la cabeza. En un cuento de ciencia ficción el hombre comprendería eventualmente que se encuentra en un universo paralelo. En una novela existencialista el no reconocimiento podría deberse, simplemente, a una sensación de extrañamiento, de absurdo. En un texto experimental el misterio quedaría sin desentrañar y la situación sería resuelta por una pirueta del lenguaje. Los editores son cada vez más exigentes y el hombre sabe, con cierta desesperación, que si no logra ubicarse rápidamente en un género corre el riesgo de permanecer dolorosa, perpetuamente inédito.

Respect for Genres

A man wakes up next to a woman he doesn't recognize. In a thriller, this could be the result of alcohol, drugs, or a blow to the head. In a science fiction story, the man would eventually understand that he exists in a parallel universe. In an existentialist novel, the lack of recognition could simply be due to a feeling of alienation, of absurdity. In an experimental text, the mystery would go unsolved and the situation be handled with the turn of a phrase. The editors become more and more demanding, and the man knows, with a sense of desperation, that if he doesn't manage to fit himself into a genre soon, he runs the risk of remaining painfully and forever unpublished.

Caníbales y exploradores

Los caníbales bailan alrededor de los exploradores. Los caníbales encienden el fuego. Los caníbales tienen la cara pintada de tres colores. Los caníbales están interesados en el corazón y el cerebro, desprecian la carne tierna de los muslos, el resto de las vísceras. Los caníbales ingieren aquellas partes del cuerpo que consideran capaces de infundir en ellos las virtudes que admiran en sus víctimas. Los caníbales se ensañan sin goce en su banquete ritual. Los caníbales visten las prendas de los exploradores. Los caníbales, una vez en Londres, pronuncian documentadas conferencias sobre los caníbales.

Cannibals and Explorers

The cannibals dance around the explorers. The cannibals light the fire. The cannibals have their faces painted in three colors. The cannibals prefer the heart and brain, disdaining the tender flesh of the thighs and the leftover intestines. The cannibals consume those parts of the body they believe will instill in them the virtues they admire in their victims. The cannibals partake of their ritual banquet without pleasure or mercy. The cannibals don the explorers' clothes. The cannibals, once in London, deliver scholarly lectures on cannibals.

La temporada de fantasmas

Se abre la temporada de fantasmas. El primer fantasma entra en un bar. El tipo que atiende la barra le ofrece un whisky. Nunca tuve oportunidad de probar la coca cola, le dice el fantasma, muy triste. Pero cuando se la traen y trata de tomársela, el líquido le atraviesa la niebla y se derrama. Pronto empezarán a llegar los turistas y el dueño del bar quiere tenerlo limpio. Al mismo tiempo, los fantasmas son la principal atracción para los clientes. Los gustos, piensa el hombre con fastidio, hay que dárselos en vida.

Ghost Season

It's the opening of ghost season. The first ghost enters a bar and the bartender offers him whisky. I never had the chance to try a Coke, the ghost tells him, with chagrin. But when he's served and takes a sip, the liquid passes right through the mist and spills. Soon the tourists will arrive and the bar owner wants everything clean. On the other hand, the ghosts are the main attraction for his customers. Annoyed, the man thinks it's best to enjoy the good things in life while you can.

Taller literario I

a Mempo Giardinelli

Su vocación por el cuento breve es indudable. Sin embargo, creemos que debe usted frecuentar más a los grandes narradores. Los tres textos que nos envió, aunque todavía imperfectos, denotan una gran vitalidad. Le rogamos pasar cuanto antes por esta redacción a retirarlos. Son exigentes y violentos, se niegan a aceptar el dictamen de nuestros asesores, es difícil, sobre todo, contentar su desmesurado apetito.

Literary Workshop I

for Mempo Giardinelli

Your zeal for the short short story is unquestionable; nevertheless, we believe you should spend more time reading the great writers. The three texts you sent us, though still flawed, possess great vitality. Please stop by our office and pick them up as soon as possible. They are demanding and unruly. They refuse to accept the evaluation of our advisory board, and to make matters worse, it is difficult to satisfy their voracious appetite.

Teóloga

En el siglo VII después de Cristo, un grupo de teólogos bávaros discute sobre el sexo de los ángeles. Obviamente, no se admite que las mujeres (por entonces ni siquiera era seguro que tuvieran alma) sean capaces de discutir materias teologales. Sin embargo, uno de ellos es una mujer hábilmente disfrazada. Afirma con mucha energía que los ángeles sólo pueden pertenecer al sexo masculino. Sabe, pero no lo dice, que entre ellos habrá mujeres disfrazadas.

Theologian

In the 7th century A.D., a group of Bavarian theologians debates the sex of angels. Obviously, no one admits that women are capable of discussing theological matters, after all, back then it was doubtful they even had a soul. Nevertheless, one of them is a cleverly disguised woman. She asserts emphatically that angels must only be male. She knows, but doesn't disclose, that among them there will be cleverly disguised women.

Robinson desafortunado

Corro hacia la playa. Si las olas hubieran dejado sobre la arena un pequeño barril de pólvora, aunque estuviese mojada, una navaja, algunos clavos, incluso una colección de pipas o unas simples tablas de madera, yo podría utlizar esos objetos para construir una novela. Qué hacer en cambio con estos párrafos mojados, con estas metáforas cubiertas de lapas y mejillones, con estos restos de otro triste naufragio literario.

Unfortunate Robinson

I run toward the beach. If only the waves had left a small barrel of gunpowder on the sand, even wet powder, or a knife, some nails, maybe even a collection of pipes, or a few simple wooden planks, I could have used those things to construct a novel. But tell me, what am I supposed to do with these soaked paragraphs, with these metaphors encrusted with barnacles and mussels, with these remains of yet another unfortunate literary shipwreck.

Zafarrancho de naufragio

En el vapor de la carrera se realiza un zafarrancho de naufragio. Se controlan los botes y los pasajeros se colocan sus salvavidas. (Los niños primero y a continuación las mujeres.) De acuerdo con las convenciones de la ficción breve, se espera que el simulacro convoque a lo real: ahora es cuando el barco debería naufragar. Sin embargo, sucede lo contrario. El simulacro lo invade todo, se apodera de las acciones, de los deseos, de las caras de la tripulación y del pasaje. El barco entero es ahora un simulacro y también el mar. Incluso yo misma finjo escribir.

Abandon Ship!

Engulfed in steam, the crew prepares for an abandon-ship drill. The lifeboats are readied and the passengers don their life jackets. (Children first, then the women.) Based on the conventions of short fiction, the drill should become reality: the ship should go down now, but instead, the opposite occurs. The simulation invades everything, controlling the actions, desires, and expressions of the crew, as well as the ship's course. In the end, the entire ship's a fake, and the sea as well. Even I myself pretend to write.

El autor y el lector

Le preguntan al autor: usted, cuando escribe, ¿piensa en el lector? El autor no piensa en otra cosa. En su pensamiento el lector es un príncipe envuelto en telas bordadas y brillantes. Su principado es una colonia de la Tierra en el espacio-exterior. Como es un príncipe, tiene gestos indolentes y gestos desdeñosos. Con un gesto desdeñoso aparta de sí la edición árabe de la obra del autor. Con un gesto indolente llama al bibliotecario del palacio y le exige la traducción al alemán. El príncipe y lector es políglota y sensible. Lee y se emociona: cómo es posible que desde tan lejos en el tiempo y el espacio, otro hombre pueda expresar así mis propios sentimientos. A todo esto, el autor no ha contestado la pregunta y se la vuelven a formular en voz más alta. Un poco sobresaltado, se apresura a contestar: no, claro que no, jamás pienso en el lector, un verdadero artista piensa solamente en su obra. Entonces el periodista se va y el autor se queda muy triste, pensando que no es un verdadero artista y que le gustaría serlo.

The Author and the Reader

The author is asked: sir, when you write, do you keep the reader in mind? The author thinks of nothing else. He envisions the reader as a prince clothed in dazzling, embroidered fabrics. His principality is a colony of the Earth in outer space. Because he's a prince, his gestures are nonchalant and cavalier. With a cavalier gesture, he casts aside the Arabic edition of the author's work. With a nonchalant gesture, he summons the palace librarian and demands the German translation. The prince is quite a linguist and a perceptive reader. He reads and is moved: how's it possible that someone from such a distant time and place can express my feelings this way? Meanwhile, the author hasn't answered the question, which is repeated to him in a louder voice. Somewhat startled, the author quickly responds: no, of course not, I never think about the reader, a true artist only thinks about his work. After the journalist leaves, the author feels sad, thinking that he's not a true artist and wishing he could be one.

III. from
Botánica del caos 🌀 *Botany of Chaos*

Amores entre guardián y casuarina

Plaza pública. Guardián enamorado de casuarina (secretamente, incluso para sí mismo). Recorte del presupuesto municipal. Guardián trasladado a tareas de oficina. Casuarina languidece. Guardián languidece. Patéticos encuentros nocturnos. Con el correr de los días, casuarina transformado en palo borracho. Murmuraciones en el barrio. Una noche, trágico parto prematuro: vástago discretamente enterrado. Previsible crecimiento in situ de una planta desclasada y rebelde que se niega a permanecer atada a sus raíces pero tampoco quiere estudiar y bebe desordenadamente cerveza sentada en el cordón de la vereda.

Romance between Guard and Magnolia

Public square. Guard in love with Magnolia (secretly, denying it even to himself). City budget cuts. Guard transferred to office job. Magnolia languishes. Guard languishes. Pathetic nocturnal encounters. With each passing day, Magnolia blossoms. Rumors in the neighborhood. One night, tragic premature birth: offspring buried discreetly. At the site, noticeable growth of a rebellious misfit sapling who refuses to remain tied to his roots, hates to study, and sits on the curb guzzling beer.

Cuidado con las mujeres

Que una mujer no tenga raíces (o finja no tenerlas) no es prueba suficiente, yo me fijaría en lo que come, en su forma de saludar (cierta flexibilidad en las reverencias), me acercaría para saber si le huelen a viento los suspiros, si tiene nudos como nidos en el pelo frondoso. Hábiles especies híbridas que pivotean entre dos reinos, estas supuestas mujeres se disfrazan, seducen, fingen amor, se reproducen al menor descuido.

Beware of Women

That a woman has no roots (or pretends not to have them) is not enough proof. I would pay attention to what she eats, how she greets others (a certain flexibility in her curtsies). I would approach her to see if her sighs smell like the wind, if she has tangles like nests in her luxuriant hair. Clever, hybrid species that flitter between two kingdoms, these deceitful women disguise themselves, seduce, pretend to love, and reproduce at the slightest provocation.

ABUELA NO NOS CREE

—¿Por qué me sacaron de mi casa? —pregunta mi abuela, los ojos extraviados.

—Ésta es tu casa, ¿ves? El empapelado con flores de lis, ¿ves? La colcha con la quemadura de cigarillo, ¿ves? La cocina verde, con la puerta de la alacena rota, ¿ves?

La abuela no ve y llora con desconsuelo.

—Me trajeron aquí para robarme mi casa.

Pero no fuimos nosotros, quisiera decirle. El tiempo ladrón te trajo aquí, y se quedó con todo.

GRANDMA DOESN'T BELIEVE US

"Why did you take me away from my house?," my grandmother asks, with vacant eyes.

"But this is your house, can't you see? See the fleur-de-lis wallpaper? See the bedspread with the cigarette burn? See the green kitchen with the broken cupboard door?"

Grandma can't see and weeps inconsolably.

"You brought me here to steal my house out from under me."

But it wasn't us, I'd like to tell her. Time was the thief who brought you here and kept everything for himself.

El padre y el hijo

Tuvo un hijo que creció hasta ser como él cuando tenía su edad. A pesar de sus esfuerzos por dejarse alcanzar, el padre había seguido adelante sin poder evitarlo. Sin embargo, a partir de cierto número de años, la ventaja que le llevaba a su hijo comenzó a convertirse en retraso.

—No te preocupes, papá—decía el hijo para consolarlo—, la vida no es una carrera.

No cuesta nada hablar así cuando se va ganando.

Father and Son

He had a son who grew up to be just like him when he was that age. Despite his efforts to let his son catch up, the father couldn't help but stay ahead. Nevertheless, after a certain number of years, the advantage he had over his son began to slip, leaving him behind.

"Don't worry, Pop," his son would say to console him, "life isn't a race."

That's easy to say when you're winning.

SI VIAJAR EN EL TIEMPO FUERA POSIBLE

Viajar en el tiempo no sólo es posible sino también obligatorio y constante. Desde que nací no hago otra cosa que navegar hacia un mal destino. Lo que quisera es poder detenerme, quedarme aquí mismo, que no se está mal: echar el ancla.

TIME TRAVEL

Time travel's not only possible but also inescapable and never ending. Ever since I was born, I've done nothing but sail toward an abominable fate. What I'd like to do is stop, stay right here, which isn't too bad: throw out the anchor.

El Día del Juicio Final

Intensamente concentrado en su programa favorito no alcanza a darse cuenta de que el resto del mundo se ha desvanecido a su alrededor, que las trompetas han sonado, que los cuatro jinetes derramaron su furia; no alcanza a darse cuenta de que ha sido definitivamente juzgado, pesadas sus buenas obras y las malas, que el fiel de la balanza se ha inclinado a su favor, que desde ahora y para siempre, intensamente concentrado en su programa favorito, está en el Paraíso.

Judgment Day

Intensely engrossed in his favorite show, he fails to notice that the rest of the world has vanished around him, that the trumpets have sounded, and the Four Horsemen have spread their fury. He fails to notice that he has been judged once and for all, that having weighed his good and bad deeds, the faithful scale has tipped in his favor, and he remains now and forevermore, intensely engrossed in his favorite show, in Heaven.

Después de Caín

Caín mata a Abel. Imposible imaginar dolor más salvaje para sus padres. Adán y Eva no se hacen reproches pero hay horror en sus miradas. Destruido en su espíritu, Adán decide no conocer a Eva nunca más: como muchos hombres después que él, no quiere traer hijos a este mundo. No estamos informados sobre lo que piensa Eva, pero podemos suponer que se somete al dolor. De día no necesitan controlarse: durante ciento cuarenta años la pena apaga el deseo. Pero de noche sus cuerpos jóvenes engendran sueños. Y los meri'im, casta diabólica, aprovechan estos sueños para engendrar con ellos (los súcubos se ocupan de Adán, los íncubos de Eva) demonios más espantosos que sus propios padres infernales, porque llevan en sí la semilla de la maldad humana, que no es inocente.

After Cain

Cain kills Abel. Hard to imagine pain more brutal for his parents. Adam and Eve don't blame each other, but there's horror in their eyes. His spirit destroyed, Adam decides never to know Eve again. Like many men after him, he doesn't want to bring more children into this world. We are not informed as to what Eve thought, but we can assume she surrendered to the pain. They don't have to restrain themselves in the waking hours: throughout one hundred and forty years, misery eclipses desire. But at night their young bodies beget dreams. And the Meri'im, a diabolical caste, enter their dreams (the succubus descend upon Adam, the incubus upon Eve) to engender them with demons more horrifying than their own infernal parents, because they carry within them the seed of human evil, which is not innocent.

EL DIOS VIEJO DEL FUEGO

a Juan Epple

Con las piedras del antiguo templo pagano dedicado al dios del fuego se construyó la iglesia.

Hoy, la iglesia está atestada. Hay, sobre todo, mujeres y algunos niños. Se han refugiado allí y han cerrado la única, enorme puerta con pesadas trabas para defenderse de sus enemigos.

El Dios Viejo del Fuego usa una de sus llamaradas para encender un cigarro de hoja. Los fieles no ven el peligro: confunden con incienso el humo que enrojece sus ojos, confunden con el brillo del sol en los vitrales el fulgor de la brasa.

El Dios del Fuego ha visto ascender y borrarse en la consideración de los hombres muchos monótonos Dioses de la Justicia. Sabe que sólo el terror y la locura perviven a través de los ritos, de las culturas, de los siglos. Usa otra de sus inmensas llamaradas para iluminar la escena a sus ojos legañosos. Es infinitamente viejo y fuma en paz. No va a molestarse en incendiar la iglesia sólo para darle el gusto al lector.

The Ancient God of Fire

to Juan Epple

The church was built with stones from the ancient pagan temple dedicated to the God of Fire. Today the church is packed, with mostly women and children. They've sought refuge there and have closed the one and only enormous door with heavy bars to defend themselves from their enemies.

The Ancient God of Fire uses one of his flames to light his cigar. The flock doesn't foresee the danger: they mistake the smoke irritating their eyes for incense, and confuse the blaze of the embers with the glow of the sun shining through the stained glass windows.

The God of Fire has seen many Gods of Justice rise and fall at the hands of mankind. He knows that only terror and madness persist in rituals and cultures throughout centuries. He uses another one of his immense flames to illuminate the scene for his sleepy eyes. He's infinitely old and smokes in peace. He's not going to bother to burn down the church just to satisfy the reader.

Información útil

En la sala de espera, los pacientes intercambian información sobre sus enfermedades. El doctor es impuntual, la espera es larga, el doctor es tacaño, no hay revistas. La secretaria se queja: hay que rehacer una y otra vez las historias clínicas cuando los pacientes, aburridos, se entretienen intercambiando enfermedades. Una noche, la señora que limpia el consultorio encuentra en el cenicero atestado de colillas una obstrucción del colédoco con la que nadie se quiso quedar.

Pertinent Information

The patients exchange information about their illnesses in the waiting room. The doctor's running behind, the wait's long, the doctor's stingy, there are no magazines. The receptionist complains that she has to update the medical histories over and over again when the patients, out of boredom, entertain themselves by trading illnesses. One night, the cleaning lady finds, in the ashtray filled with cigarette butts, an obstruction of the bile duct no one wanted to keep.

Los auxilios de la medicina

Mi señora siempre tan terca, doctor. Pero a usted lo respeta. Convénzala, por favor, de que se quede quieta, de que no se levante descalza en mitad de la noche, de que no revolee los ojos delante de las visitas; convénzala usted, que tiene influencia sobre ella, de que los muertos verdaderos no se mueven ni se quejan, o bien no están muertos del todo, pero por favor, que se decida de una vez, doctor.

Medical Assistance

My wife, always so stubborn, Doctor. But she respects you. Convince her, please, to stay still, and not get up barefoot in the middle of the night, and roll her eyes at the guests. Convince her, Doctor, she'll listen to you, that real corpses don't move or complain, or if they do, they're not really dead. But please, Doctor, help her make up her mind once and for all.

Profetas y cataclismos IV

Lo echaron de la ciudad cuando se cumplió su profecía. Había anunciado abundancia, buenas cosechas, alegría. Sólo entonces entendió que los hombres creen ser los únicos hacedores de su propia dicha pero no admiten responsabilidad en su desgracia. Desde entonces sólo anuncia calamidades. Lo recompensan todavía mejor cuando no se cumplen.

Prophets and Catastrophes IV

They banished him from the city when his prophecy came true. He had predicted abundance, good harvests, happiness. Only then did he understand that people take all the credit for their good fortune but won't own up to their rotten luck. Since then, he only foretells calamities. He gets paid even more when they don't come to pass.

Profetas y cataclismos VI

El éxito de sus palabras hizo fracasar su misión. La profecía fue escuchada y reconocida. Los hombres cambiaron su conducta impía y se evitó el fuego y el azufre, se evitó el pánico y el horror, no sucedió la lluvia de la muerte. Así, por falta de cataclismo, jamás logró acceder al rango de profeta ni pudo el Más Alto mostrarse en todo su poder. Sólo se envían desde entonces profetas monótonos o tartamudos, débiles en el arte de la oratoria: es importante, sobre todo, que carezcan de carisma personal.

Prophets and Catastrophes VI

The success of his words made his mission fail. The prophecy was heeded and appreciated. The people changed their irreverent behavior and avoided fire and sulfur, panic and horror. Nor did the rain of death come to pass. Thus, for lack of catastrophes, he never made it to the rank of prophet, nor was the Almighty able to demonstrate his true powers. Since then, they only send boring or stammering prophets, weak in the art of public speaking, and above all, lacking personal charisma.

ALÍ BABÁ

Qué absurda, qué incomprensible me parecía cuando era chica la confusión del hermano de Alí Babá: casi un error técnico, una manifiesta falta de verosimilitud. Encerrado en la cueva de los cuarenta ladrones, ¿cómo era posible que no lograra recordar la fórmula mágica, el simple ábrete-sésamo que le hubiera servido para abrir la puerta, para salvar su vida?

Y aquí estoy, tantos años después, en peligro yo misma, tipeando desesperadamente en el tablero de mi computadora, sin recordar la exacta combinación de letras que podría darme acceso a la salvación: ábrete cardamomo, ábrete centeno, ábrete maldita semilla de ajonjolí.

ALI BABA

When I was a little girl, it seemed so absurd, so incomprehensible to me that Ali Baba's brother could become so confused and make such a silly, absolutely unbelievable mistake. Locked inside the cave of the forty thieves, how was it possible he couldn't remember the magic formula, the simple "open sesame" that would've opened the door for him and saved his life?

And here I am, so many years later, in danger myself, typing desperately on my computer keyboard, unable to remember the exact combination of letters that could lead to my salvation: "Open cardamon, open rye, open up, you damn sesame seed!"

En el avión

Hace calor, estamos atados a nuestros asientos, no hay espacio para extender las piernas. Esperamos, contra toda lógica, que el avión levante vuelo, confiamos como niños en que la pesadísima construcción de acero correrá locamente por la pista hasta echarse a volar. Sólo los desconfiados, los intensos, los verdaderamente adultos somos capaces de ver la figura del enorme pájaro Roc que toma el avión entre sus garras y nos eleva sobre las nubes de una manera tanto más razonable, más explicable, más sensata.

On the Plane

It's hot. We're strapped into our seats and there's no room to stretch our legs. We wait against all logic for the plane to take off. Like children, we have faith that this extremely heavy metal object will taxi like crazy down the runway until it lifts off. Only the wary among us, the perceptive, the real grown-ups, are capable of seeing the silhouette of the gigantic bird Roc take the plane between its talons and lift us above the clouds in a way that's so much more reasonable, understandable, and practical.

Por falta de pruebas

Saltos enormes, de veinte o treinta metros de largo en los que me elevo por encima de las copas de los árboles y sin embargo son sólo eso, saltos: la prueba cruel de que no levanto vuelo.

For Lack of Proof

Enormous leaps, sixty or ninety feet high, in which I soar above the tree tops, and yet that's all they are, leaps: the devastating proof that I can't fly.

Con alivio

Prefiero la muerte a la tortura. Con uno de los trozos de vidrio me tajeo el cuello. Es una herida profunda. La vida sale casi de golpe, con la sangre. Siento alivio, por fin me estoy vaciando. Todo lo anterior, por suerte, lo he olvidado al despertar.

What a Relief

I prefer death to torture. I slash my throat with one of the shards of glass. It's a deep wound. Life escapes me almost instantly, along with the blood. I feel relieved that I'm almost empty. Fortunately, when I awake, I've forgotten everything that ever happened before.

La más absoluta certeza

Pocas certezas es posible atesorar en este mundo. Por ejemplo, Marco Denevi duda con ingenio de la existencia de los chinos. Y sin embargo yo sé que en este momento usted, una persona a la que no puedo ver, a la que no conozco ni imagino, una persona cuya realidad (fuera de este pequeño acto que nos compete) me es completamente indiferente, cuya existencia habré olvidado apenas termine de escribir estas líneas, usted, ahora, con la más absoluta certeza, está leyendo.

Most Absolute Certainty

We can hardly be sure of anything in this world. For example, in his ingenious story, Marco Denevi casts doubt on the existence of the Chinese. And yet I know at this very moment that you, a person I can't see, someone I don't know or can't imagine, a person whose reality means absolutely nothing to me (outside this small act that unites us), and whose existence I'll have forgotten as soon as I finish writing these lines, you, with most absolute certainty, are reading now.

Lo que pudo ser

A ella le hubiera gustado su nariz porque parecía tallada con un cuchillo viejo, un poco desafilado, que no servía para tallar. A él le gustaba el cognac. De ella le hubieran gustado las tetas y la forma de mirar, fuerte y distraída al mismo tiempo, como si desafiara a una persona invisible o ausente. Pero como no eran personajes de la misma historia, nunca llegaron a conocerse. Vaya usted a saber los amores que nos perdemos cada día por culpa de nuestro autor.

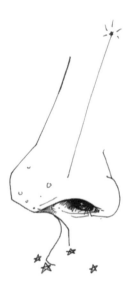

What Could Have Been

She would have liked his nose because it seemed sculpted with an old knife, slightly dull, unfit for carving. He had a fondness for cognac and would have liked her boobs and that way she had of staring, intensely and distractedly at the same time, as if confronting someone invisible or absent. But because they weren't characters in the same story, they never met each other. Who knows how many loves we miss out on each day because of our author.

Ese gato

Ese gato parece una persona por la mirada inteligente de sus ojos, porque sabe pararse en dos patitas, por la forma en que desdeña el alimento balanceado y se sienta a la mesa como un comensal más para devorar no sólo la carne sino el pan y la ensalada.

Parece una persona porque se sirve de sus garras casi como si fueran manos, porque lo visten de esa manera absurda, con un jean azul y la camisa a cuadros.

A tal punto parece una persona que necesito mirarlo fijamente y repetirme una y otra vez: es un gato es un gato es un gato es un gato es un gato, mientras me pregunto cuándo me devolverá los dólares que le presté el mes pasado.

That Cat

That cat seems like a person because of the intelligent look in his eyes, because he knows how to stand on two legs, because of the way he disdains a balanced diet and sits at the table like any other guest to devour not only meat but also bread and salad.

He seems like a person because he eats with his paws as if they were hands, because they dress him in that ridiculous manner, in blue jeans and a plaid shirt.

He looks so much like a person that I need to stare at him and repeat to myself over and over: it's a cat it's a cat it's a cat it's a cat it's a cat, while I wonder when he's going to return the money I loaned him last month.

Tabú cultural

A causa de algún tabú cultural que aún no comprendemos, los nativos no quieren aceptar la colaboración de nuestros científicos para averiguar por qué se malogra, una y otra vez, la cosecha de humanos en esos campos sembrados que llaman cementerios. ¡Cuando sería tan sencillo lograr que fructifique!

Cultural Taboo

Due to some cultural taboo we have yet to understand, the natives refuse to accept the collaboration of our scientists to determine why, time and time again, the harvest of humans goes to waste in those cultivated fields they call cemeteries. When it would be so easy to make them bear fruit!

Desnudez

Quien visite por primera vez nuestro mundo podría pensar que
la vestimenta que nos cubre es parte natural de nuestros cuerpos,
que la piel, esta carne, estos huesos, son permanentes; podría
suponer, el visitante, que no podemos librarnos de ellos, reem-
plazarlos por otra piel, carne más nueva, más colorida, otros hue-
sos o ninguno en esa desnudez total con la que (sólo en privado)
dejamos de vernos en los espejos.

Nudity

Whoever visits our world for the first time might think the
apparel covering us is a natural part of our bodies, that our skin,
this flesh, these bones, are permanent. Our visitor might assume
we can't free ourselves from them, replace them with other skin,
or with newer and brighter flesh, with other bones, or none at all
in that total nudity in which (only in private) we no longer see
ourselves in the mirror.

MAGO QUE CREE EN SU MAGIA

El mago conoce todos sus trucos y sin embargo cree en su propia magia, al punto de intentar el vuelo muchas veces. Con varios huesos rotos pero la ilusión intacta, sabe que estar vivo es un milagro y se lo atribuye alegremente.

THE MAGICIAN WHO BELIEVES IN MAGIC

The magician knows all his tricks and yet he believes in his own magic so much that he's tried to fly many times. With several broken bones, but with his enthusiasm still intact, he knows that just being alive is a miracle and gladly takes credit for it.

El insuperable arte de Ma Liang

Ma Liang fue un legendario pintor chino cuya imitación del mundo era tan perfecta que podía transformarse en realidad con la pincelada final. Un emperador le exigió que pintara el océano y en él se ahogó con toda su corte.

Para superar el arte de Ma Liang, Occidente inventó la fotografía y después el cine, donde sobreviven los muertos repitiendo una y otra vez los mismos actos, como en cualquier otro infierno.

The Unsurpassable Art of Ma Liang

Ma Liang was a legendary Chinese painter whose imitation of the world was so perfect he could transform it into reality with the final stroke of his brush. An emperor, who demanded he paint the ocean, drowned in it, along with his entire court.

To surpass the art of Ma Liang, the West invented photography, and later movies, in which the dead survive, repeating the same acts over and over again, as in any other Hell.

Malos consejos

Por consejo del hechicero, talló una figura de madera con la forma exacta de su enemigo. La quemó en el campo, de noche, bajo la luna. Atraído por el resplandor de la hoguera, su enemigo lo descubrió y lo mató de un lanzazo.

Bad Advice

Following the sorcerer's advice, he carved a wooden figure in the exact image of his enemy and burned it in a field, at night, under the moon. Attracted by the glow of the bonfire, his enemy found him and killed him with one thrust of his spear.

Excesos de pasión

Nos amamos frenéticamente fundiendo nuestros cuerpos en uno. Sólo nuestros documentos de identidad prueban ahora que alguna vez fuimos dos y aun así enfrentamos dificultades: la planilla de impuestos, los parientes, la incómoda circunstancia de que nuestros gustos no coinciden tanto como creíamos.

Excesses of Passion

We loved each other madly, fusing our bodies in one. Now only our ID's prove we were once two, and yet we still have challenges to face: the tax forms, the relatives, the distressing fact that we don't have as much in common as we thought.

Hombre sobre la alfombra

Luis ve al hombre en el suelo, le parece que está muerto y lo dice.

—Se murió.

—No —dice la mamá—. Se quedó dormido.

—Nadie se duerme así tirado. Es incómodo —dice Luis.

—Estaba muy cansado. Yo también a veces me quedaría dormida: ¡exactamente así!

Luis y su mamá tendrían que hablar en voz más baja, porque el hombre no está muerto ni dormido sino dibujado en un libro, y oye perfectamente todo lo que dicen de él.

Man on the Rug

Luis sees a man on the floor and says he thinks he's dead. "He died."

"No," his mother says, "he just fell asleep."

"Nobody falls asleep laying that way. It's uncomfortable," says Luis.

"He was very tired. Sometimes I too would like to fall asleep just like that!"

Luis and his mother ought to lower their voices because the man's not dead or asleep, but illustrated in a book, and hears perfectly well everything they're saying about him.

Vuelo de libertad

Abrí su jaula, y a través de la ventana de la torre lo lancé hacia la vida. ¡A volar!, le dije. Pero quien nace prisionero le teme a la libertad. Me lo recordó, desesperado, su ladrido final.

Flight of Freedom

I opened his cage and threw him from the tower window toward life. Fly! I told him. But natural born prisoners fear freedom. I was reminded of that by his final desperate bark.

Próceres en el pizarrón
Alicia Susana Estrada dibujaba muy bien a los próceres de perfil. Pero cuando se daban vuelta y nos miraban se notaba que todas las caras le habían salido parecidas.

Founding Fathers on the Blackboard
Alicia Susana Estrada could draw the profiles of the founding fathers very well, but when they turned and looked at us, it was obvious their faces had all come out the same.

IV. from
Temporada de fantasmas ℘ *Ghost Season*

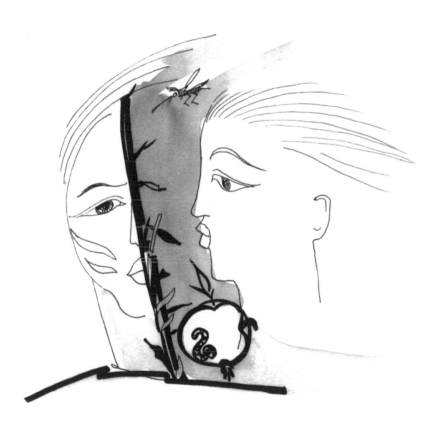

Temporada de fantasmas

No vienen a buscar pareja, ni para desovar. No necesitan reproducirse. Tampoco es posible cazarlos. No tienen entidad suficiente para caer en las redes de la lógica, los atraviesan las balas de la razón. Breves, esenciales, despojados de su carne, vienen aquí a mostrarse, vienen para agitar ante los observadores sus húmedos sudarios. Y sin embargo, no se exhiben ante los ojos de cualquiera. El experto observador de fantasmas sabe que debe optar por una mirada indiferente, nunca directa, aceptar esa percepción imprecisa, de costado, sin tratar de apropiarse de un significado evanescente que se deshace entre los dedos: textos translúcidos, medusas del sentido.

Se abre la Temporada de Fantasmas.

Ghost Season

They don't come to mate or lay eggs. They don't need to reproduce, nor is it possible to hunt them. They're too intangible to be captured in the nets of logic, and the bullets of reason pass right through them. Ephemeral, unadorned, stripped of their flesh, they come here to be seen, they come to flutter their damp shrouds at observers, and yet, they don't expose themselves to just anyone. Expert ghostwatchers know they should observe with an indifferent gaze, never a direct one, and accept that incorporeal vision, out of the corner of the eye, without trying to seize a fleeting substance that disintegrates between their fingers: translucent texts, medusas of meaning.

It's the opening of Ghost Season.

Concatenación

Los acontecimientos del pasado son los que determinan el presente. Por ejemplo, si tus padres no se hubieran conocido, hoy no existirías. Cuanto más se retrocede en el encadenamiento de circunstancias que conforman la historia del mundo, más inesperadas y sutiles serán las consecuencias que acarree el hecho más nimio, en una compleja, casi infinita sucesión de concatenaciones. Por ejemplo, si durante el cretásico superior cierto plesiosaurio carnívoro no se hubiera comido los huevos que una hembra de triceratops desovó tontamente cerca de la orilla, quizás, vaya uno a saber, me seguirías queriendo.

Concatenation

The events of the past determine those of the present. For example, if your parents hadn't met, you wouldn't exist today. The further back you go in the chain of circumstances that shape the history of the world, the more surprising and subtle the consequences of the most trivial act become, resulting in a complex, almost infinite series of concatenations. For example, if during the Late Cretaceous Period a certain carnivorous plesiosaurus hadn't eaten the eggs that a female triceratops had foolishly laid on the shoreline, perhaps, who knows, you'd still love me.

Su viuda y su voz

De las cañerías provenía un ruido fuerte y triste al que ella suponía la voz de su marido muerto. Todas las cañerías hacen ruido, argumentaban sus amigos. En todas las cañerías se manifiesta su espíritu, decía ella. Todas las cañerías hacían ruido cuando él estaba entre nosotros, argumentaban sus amigos. Pero solamente ahora me hablan de amor, decía ella.

His Widow and his Voice

From the pipes there arose a loud and sad noise, which she believed to be the voice of her dead husband. All of the pipes make noise, her friends argued. His spirit reveals itself in all of the pipes, she said. All of the pipes made noise when he was with us, her friends insisted. But only now do they speak to me of love, she replied.

El niño terco

En un apartado de su obra dedicado a las leyendas infantiles, los hermanos Grimm refieren un cuento popular alemán que la sensibilidad de la época consideraba particularmente adecuado para los niños. Un niño terco fue castigado por el Señor con la enfermedad y la muerte. Pero ni aun así logró enmendarse. Su bracito pálido, con la mano como una flor abierta, insistía en asomar fuera de la tumba. Sólo cuando su madre le dio una buena tunda con una vara de avellano, el bracito se retiró otra vez bajo tierra y fue la prueba de que el niño había alcanzado la paz.

Los que hemos pasado por ese cementerio, sabemos, sin embargo, que se sigue asomando cuando cree que nadie lo ve. Ahora es el brazo recio y peludo de un hombre adulto, con los dedos agrietados y las uñas sucias de tierra por el trabajo de abrirse paso hacia abajo y hacia arriba. A veces hace gestos obscenos, curiosamente modernos, que los filólogos consideran dirigidos a los hermanos Grimm.

The Stubborn Boy

In a section of their work dedicated to children's legends, the Brothers Grimm refer to a popular German story that in its time was considered an appropriate cautionary tale for children. A stubborn boy was punished by God with illness and death, but after all that, he still didn't mend his ways. His pale little arm, with its hand like an open flower, would poke out of the grave time and time again. Only when his mother gave him a good swat with a hazelnut stick, did his little arm slip below the earth again, proof that the child had found peace.

Those of us who have passed by that cemetery know, however, that it still creeps out whenever he thinks no one's looking. Now it's the strong and hairy arm of an adult man, with fingers cracked and nails encrusted with dirt from struggling to force its way up and down. Sometimes the hand makes obscene gestures, surprisingly modern ones, which philologists assume are meant for the Brothers Grimm.

La ardilla verosímil

Un hombre es amigo de una ardilla que vive en el jardín de un conocido financista. Trepando de un salto al alféizar de la ventana, la ardilla escucha conversaciones claves acerca de las oscilaciones de la Bolsa de Valores. Usted no se sorprenderá en absoluto si le cuento que el amigo de la ardilla se enriquece rápidamente con sus inversiones.

Pero yo sí estoy sorprendida. No dejo de preguntarme por qué usted está tan dispuesto a creer, sin un instante de duda, que una ardilla pueda entender conversaciones claves acera de las oscilaciones de la Bolsa.

The Trusty Squirrel

A man is friends with a squirrel that lives in the garden of a successful investor. Springing to the windowsill in one leap, the squirrel overhears vital conversations about fluctuations in the Stock Market. You wouldn't be the least bit surprised if I told you that the squirrel's friend got rich quick from his investments.

But frankly I'm amazed. I can't help but wonder why you're so willing to believe, without doubting for an instant, that a squirrel can understand vital conversations about fluctuations in the Stock Market.

El pájaro azul

Un hombre persigue al Pájaro de la Felicidad durante meses y
años, a través de nueve montañas y nueve ríos, venciendo endria-
gos y tentaciones, tolerando llagas y desdichas. Antepone la
búsqueda del Pájaro a toda otra ambición, necesidad o deseo. El
tiempo pasa y pesa sobre sus hombros, pero también el Pájaro
envejece, sus plumas se decoloran y ralean.

Lo atrapa en un día frío, desgraciado. El anciano está hambri-
ento. El Pájaro está flaco pero es carne. Le arranca sus plumas
todavía azules con cuidado, lo espeta en el asador y se lo come.
Ahora se siente satisfecho, brevemente feliz.

The Blue Bird of Happiness

A man pursues the Blue Bird of Happiness for months, for
years, over nine mountains and nine rivers, conquering beasts and
temptations, enduring wounds and tribulations. He places his
quest for the Bird above all other ambitions, needs, or desires.
Time passes and weighs heavily on his shoulders, but the Bird
also grows old, its feathers lose their color and fall out.

He captures it one cold, unfortunate day. The old man's starv-
ing. The Bird's skinny, but edible. He plucks out the remaining
blue feathers carefully, skewers it over the flame, and then devours
it. Now he feels content, happy for an instant.

Hombre que huye

Para detener a la bruja que lo persigue, arroja un peine y el peine se convierte en bosque. Jadeando, la bruja atraviesa el bosque y los árboles se inclinan con la fuerza de su aliento. Entonces el hombre arroja una piedra, y la piedra se convierte en una montaña. Jadeando, la bruja trepa la montaña, y provoca avalanchas la fuerza de su aliento. El hombre deja caer una lágrima y la lágrima se convierte en un lago. Pero la bruja se inclina sobre el agua y se bebe el lago hasta dejarlo seco. Después atrapa a su marido y se lo lleva otra vez para la casa, es hora de cenar y no de andar correteando ninfas.

Man on the Run

In order to stop the witch who's pursuing him, he throws a comb at her and the comb becomes a forest. Panting, the witch crosses the forest and the trees bend under the force of her breath. Then the man throws a stone and the stone becomes a mountain. Gasping, the witch climbs the mountain and her powerful breath sets off avalanches. The man allows a tear to fall and the tear becomes a lake, but the witch bends over the water and drinks up the lake, leaving it bone dry. Then once again she captures her husband and takes him back home; it's time for dinner, not for chasing after nymphs.

Los corredores

A los más veloces los llaman liebres. Su vida está dedicada a la carrera. Se afeitan todo el cuerpo para reducir la fricción del aire. Se untan con glicerina las tetillas para no lastimarse con el roce de la ropa. Mientras corren, absorben un líquido espeso cargado de carbohidratos y minerales, que llevan en pequeños envases descartables. Y sin embargo la meta está siempre más lejos, huye hacia adelante, nunca podrán alcanzarla, tal como nos pasa a todos, incluso a los más lentos.

Runners

The fastest runners are called hares. They live to run. They shave their entire body to decrease wind resistance, and anoint their nipples with Vaseline to avoid chafing from the rubbing of their shirts. On the run, they absorb a thick liquid loaded with carbohydrates and minerals, which they carry in small disposable containers. And yet, the goal is always off in the distance, scurrying ahead of them. They'll never be able to catch up with it. The same goes for the rest of us, even the slowest.

Una confesión

No vale la pena que le pregunte a mi prima, ella siempre me lleva la contra. Si le digo que fui yo por algo será. ¿Acaso me conviene ir a la cárcel? Será nomás porque necesito castigo aquí, en este mundo, para que no me castiguen después del otro lado. Pero a mi prima, ya se lo dije, no le pregunte, porque no le va a decir nada, con esa carita de idiota, con esa manía de no contestar cuando le hablan que siempre me ponía loca, ya va a ver cuando se quede así, sin moverse, tan callada, tan fría, si no le dan ganas de matarla a usted también.

A Confession

Don't waste your time asking my cousin, she always contradicts me. If I tell you I did it, there must be a reason. Maybe it's worth going to jail? That way, if they punish me here, in this world, they won't have to punish me later, in the next one. But I already told you, don't bother asking my cousin because she's not going to tell you anything, with that stupid face, and that habit of hers of not answering whenever you talk to her, which always drove me crazy, you'll see for yourself when she just lays there, without moving, so quiet, so cold, if you don't feel like killing her too.

La persecución

La luz verde provoca una estampida. La manada te persigue. Es inútil correr hacia adelante, son más veloces que cualquier humano, tienen más resistencia. Doblar no es mala idea, pero muchos doblan detrás tuyo. Has leído en los diarios casos infrecuentes pero ciertos de vehículos que no trepidan en subir a la vereda para rematar a sus víctimas, a costa de dañar sus propias extremidades.

Es preferible recluirse. Que te saquen de tu casa entre varios sólo cuando cruzar la calle sea imprescindible para llegar (a su propio riesgo) al cementerio.

The Hunt

The green light sets off a stampede and the herd chases you. It's useless to run ahead of them, they're faster and stronger than any human. Turning isn't a bad idea, but many turn to follow you. Although it seldom happens, you've read in the paper about true cases of vehicles that don't hesitate jumping the curb to finish off their victims on the sidewalk, at the expense of damaging their own parts.

It's best to stay inside. Let them come and carry you out of your house only when crossing the street becomes absolutely necessary for you to make it (at their own risk) to the cemetery.

El Murciélago

Jorge tiene ochenta y cuatro años, pero cuando habla no es un viejo. Es aquel muchacho que vivió su adolescencia en Justiniano Posse, provincia de Córdoba. Allí supo tener una Norton, una moto de 125 cc. con la que viajaba a otros pueblos los sábados a la noche para bailar con la orquesta de Malherba, o la del maestro Brunelli.

Un día cambió la moto por un Ford modelo 31 en estado de destrucción. Al autito lo llamaban *El Murciélago*, porque sólo salía de noche. Los viajantes solían dejar sus autos en la playa de la estación del servicio. A la madrugada, un mecánico amigo les sacaba las piezas que necesitaba el Fordcito de repuesto y les dejaba las viejas. *El Murciélago* era caníbal.

Quién tuviera hoy, piensa Jorge y no lo dice, un médico tan amigo, tan confiable.

The Bat

Jorge is eighty-four years old, but when he speaks he's not an old man. He's that boy who grew up in Justiniano Posse in the province of Córdoba. There he was known for his Norton, a 125 cc. motorcycle he'd ride to other towns on Saturday nights to dance to the Malherba Orchestra or Master Brunelli's band.

One day he traded the motorcycle for a rundown 1931 Model A Ford. The car was nicknamed *The Bat* because it only ventured out at night. The salesmen would leave their cars in the gas station parking lot, and at dawn, a mechanic friend of Jorge's would confiscate the parts that his beloved Ford needed, and replace them with the old ones. *The Bat* was a cannibal.

If only I had today, Jorge thinks to himself, a doctor who was such a trustworthy friend.

LA PROFESIONAL

Siempre te dicen que has sido la Reina de Saba, o Cleopatra. Nunca una panadera, una costurera, una lavandera de la época de la Reina de Saba. O la manicura de Cleopatra, que ya sería honor, alta jerarquía. No les hagas caso. Fuiste una espiga de centeno en un mar de cereal, olas al viento, fuiste una abeja más en el enjambre, fuiste madre en cuarenta y siete de tus vidas pasadas y cada vez tuviste muchos hijos. Pero lo que importa es el futuro. Serás la mujer que abra su cartera, serás la que me entregue un crujiente billete de cien dólares cuando abandone mi pose y mi silencio, cuando deje de mirar la pirámide de acrílico y te diga, con mis ojos clavados en tus ojos: siento, presiento, veo, que has sido hace miles de años Cleopatra, la amada de Julio César, la amante de Marco Antonio, la única, la incomparable, la que paga sus deudas, Cleopatra.

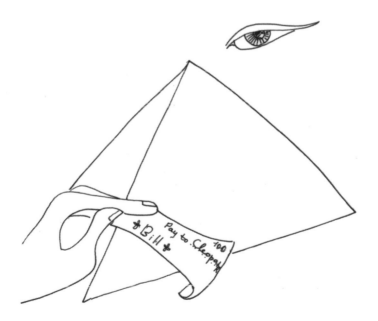

The Professional

They always tell you that you were once the Queen of Sheba, or Cleopatra. Never a baker, a seamstress, a laundrywoman from the time of the Queen of Sheba. Or Cleopatra's manicurist, which would be an honor of the highest magnitude. Don't pay attention to them. You were once a rye spike waving in the wind amidst a sea of grains, you were just another bee in the swarm, you were a mother in forty-seven of your past lives and in each one you had many children. But what really matters is the future. You will be the woman who opens her wallet, the one who hands over a crisp one-hundred-dollar bill to me when I abandon my pose and my silence, when I stop staring at the acrylic pyramid and say to you, with my eyes fixed on your eyes: I feel, I sense, I see, that thousands of years ago you were Cleopatra, the sweetheart of Julius Caesar, the lover of Mark Anthony, the one and only, the incomparable, the woman who pays her debts, Cleopatra.

Creación I: la construcción del universo

Seis millones de eones tardó en construirse el universo verdadero. El nuestro es sólo un proyecto, la maqueta a escala que el gran arquitecto armó en una semana para presentar a los inversores.

El universo terminado es muchísimo más grande, por supuesto, y más prolijo. En lugar de esta representación torpe, hay una infinita perfección en el detalle.

Y sin embargo, como siempre, los inversores se sienten engañados. Como siempre, realizar el proyecto llevó más tiempo, más esfuerzo, más inversión de lo que se había calculado. Como siempre, recuerdan con nostalgia esa torpe gracia indefinible de la maqueta que usaron para engañarlos. No deberíamos quejarnos.

Creation I: The Making of the Universe

It took six million aeons to create the real universe. Ours is just a proposal, a scaled-down model that the Great Architect erected in one week to present to the investors.

The finished universe is so much larger, of course, and more meticulous. Instead of this crude likeness, there is infinite perfection in each detail, and yet, as always, the investors feel deceived. As always, the completion of the project took more time, more effort, more money than anticipated. As always, they remember with nostalgia that elusive unrefined grace of the model used to deceive them. We shouldn't complain.

Una prueba de fe

—Yo no robé nada. En la bolsa del mercader, las monedas de oro se han convertido en aire. Quien se atreva a insinuar que no es posible, estará contradiciendo la omnipotencia de Alá.

Así dice el ladrón para comprometer a la víctima y al juez y evitar el castigo.

—Te cortaremos la mano—ordena el cadí—. Pero no como castigo sino como una prueba de fe. Alá, que todo lo puede, hará que te vuelva a crecer si eres inocente.

El ladrón es culpable. Pero Aquel que, en efecto, Todo lo Puede, hace crecer su mano de todos modos. ¿Por qué debería El Más Grande someterse a las pruebas de un cadí?

Test of Faith

"I stole nothing. Inside the merchant's bag, the gold coins have turned into thin air. Whosoever dares suggest that this is not possible challenges the omnipotence of Allah."

So says the thief to discredit the victim and the judge, and escape punishment.

"We will cut off your hand," orders the judge, "not as punishment, but rather as a test of faith. Allah, who is almighty, will make it grow back if you are innocent."

The thief is guilty. But He, in fact, Who Is Almighty, makes his hand grow back anyway. Why should The Greatest One submit to the challenge of a judge?

Mirando enfermedades

En el diccionario de Agronomía y Veterinaria había ilustraciones y muchas fotos. Una extraña tumoración nudosa deformaba la articulación de una rama.

—¿Esto qué es?—preguntaba yo, la niña.

—Es una enfermedad de los árboles —me decía papá.

—¿Esto qué es?—preguntaba yo, señalando, en la foto, el sexo de un toro.

—Es una enfermedad de las vacas —me decía papá.

Era lindo mirar enfermedades con mi papá. Como sabía que me estaba mintiendo, observaba con asombro y regocijo los desmesurados genitales que crecían deformes en los árboles machos.

Contemplating Diseases

In a dictionary of agronomy and veterinary sciences, I saw illustrations and many photographs. The joint of a branch was deformed by a strange gnarly tumor.

"What's this?" I asked when I was a little girl.

"It's a disease that trees get," Daddy told me.

"What's this?" I asked, pointing at the photo of a bull's penis.

"It's a disease that bulls get," Daddy told me.

It was fun looking at diseases with my dad. Because I knew he was lying to me, I gazed with amazement and glee at the enormous deformed genitals growing on the male trees.

Interrogatorio clínico

—¿Ha notado cambios en su funcionamiento digestivo?

—El problema es el estómago, doctor, ahora se cierra temprano.

—¿Quiere decir que a partir de cierta hora . . .?

—Ensaya allí un conjunto de música coral, es terrible.

—¿Desafina?

—Más de lo que cabe imaginar.

—¿Conoce usted al director?

—No creo que lo tengan, doctor.

—Pero habrá alguien, un representante, uno de los solistas. Sólo se trata de ponerse de acuerdo en los horarios de sus comidas.

—Los horarios no me importan, doctor. Si pudiera darme usted a tragar un frasco de buenas sopranos. . .

Medical Diagnosis

"Have you noticed any changes in your digestive system?"

"The problem is my stomach, Doctor, it shuts down early now."

"Do you mean after a certain hour?"

"A musical chorus practices there. It's terrible."

"Are they out of tune?"

"Worse than you can imagine."

"Do you know the conductor?"

"I don't think they have one, Doctor."

"But there must be someone, a representative, one of the soloists. All you have to do is get them to respect mealtimes."

"I'm not worried about my schedule, Doctor. If only you could give me a vial of good sopranos to swallow. . ."

En la silla de ruedas

Tía Petra se finge paralítica para vivir en su silla de ruedas, tapada con una manta escocesa que oculta sus patas de cabra, su cola de pez, su mitad serpiente. Los sobrinos le quitamos la manta mientras dormía y vimos las dos piernas de niño, pequeñas y delgadas, que siempre se pone para dormir.

In the Wheelchair

Aunt Petra pretends to be paralyzed so she can live in her wheelchair, wrapped in a plaid blanket that hides her goat hoofs, her fish tail, her snake bottom. My cousins and I took the blanket off Aunt Petra while she was sleeping, and we saw the two skinny little child legs she puts on whenever she takes a nap.

La desmemoria

Para disimular que ya no los recuerda, evita citar nombres propios. Para disimular que no reconoce las caras, trata a los hombres como si fueran íntimos amigos. Observa constantemente a los demás imitando con un segundo de atraso sus gestos y sus acciones. Su mundo es frágil, extranjero, desolado, pero tiene, sin embargo, algunas compensaciones. Nadie más puede tomar cada noche a una mujer distinta con la que está casado (dice ella) desde hace veinte años.

Forgetfulness

To conceal he no longer remembers them, he avoids using their names. To conceal he no longer recognizes their faces, he treats men as if they were close friends. He observes others constantly and imitates their gestures and actions with a one-second delay. His world is fragile, strange, and lonely, but on the other hand, it has its advantages. No one else can sleep each night with a different woman who claims to have been married to him for twenty years.

La caída del mundo

Los indios kogi o cogui vivían sobre la falla de Bucaramanga-Santa Marta, en Colombia. Su inestable supervivencia estaba amenazada por constantes movimientos sísmicos. Para ellos, el mundo era un huevo grande y pesado sostenido sobre cuatro vigas por cuatro hombres forzudos. Cada vez que uno de los porteadores, agotado, cambiaba la viga de un hombro al otro, se producía un terremoto. Para preservar el precario equilibrio de ese frágil universo, los indios kogi tenían prohibido saltar, gritar, tirar piedras, o que las mujeres se movieran durante el acto sexual.

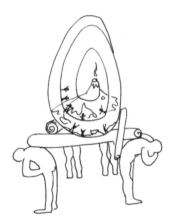

On Shaky Ground

The Kogi or Cogui Indians lived along the Bucaramanga-Santa Marta Fault in Colombia. Their shaky survival was threatened by constant seismic activity. For them, the world was an enormous heavy egg sustained on four beams by four muscular men. Each time one of the exhausted bearers would switch the beam from one shoulder to the other, an earthquake occurred. To preserve the precarious balance of that fragile universe, the Kogi Indians outlawed jumping, shouting, throwing stones, and women moving during sex.

Por única vez

Zeus, transmutado en cisne, seduce a Leda.

Después, más de cuatro cisnes muertos por asfixia desde aquel instante de goce perfecto, de goce divino, que Leda insiste inutilmente en recrear.

One Time Only

Zeus, transformed into a swan, seduces Leda.

Afterwards, more than four swans dead from asphyxiation since that instant of perfect pleasure, of divine bliss that Leda insists on recreating in vain.

CASA PRESTADA

Me han prestado su casa y yo la he perdido, qué vergüenza, qué vergüenza, cómo presentarme otra vez ante esta gente, me van a querer matar. Recorro sin suerte las calles de la ciudad, veo que faltan varias casas que han sido arrancadas de raíz, como si fueran muelas, quedan apenas pozos sanguinolentos, encías devastadas. ¿Quién soy yo? Alguien que tiene miedo de no despertar si lo matan en sueños. Casa, casa, dónde estás. Y la encuentro, de pronto, toda ella alrededor de mí, muy cerca, por suerte, de la almohada.

BORROWED HOUSE

They lent me their house and I've lost it. How embarrassing, how embarrassing! How will I ever face them again? They'll want to kill me. I scour the streets of the city with no luck. I notice several houses are missing as if they've been pulled out by their roots like molars, leaving behind only bloody holes and demolished gums. Who am I? Someone who's afraid of not waking up if they kill me in my dreams. House, house, where are you? Then suddenly I find it, completely surrounding me, very close to my pillow, lucky for me.

La ciudad soñada

Usted llega, por fin, a la ciudad soñada, pero la ciudad ya no está allí. En su lugar se eleva una cadena montañosa de indudables atractivos turísticos. Pero usted no trajo su equipo de andinista, no tiene grampas, ni cables, ni vituallas, usted trajo una guía de restaurantes y un buen traje, y entradas para el teatro. La ciudad, por el momento, está del otro lado, y el guía le ofrece atravesar la cordillera a lomo de mula. Y mientras avanza lentamente sintiendo que su columna vertebral, que sus riñones ya no están para esos trotes, usted percibe en la reverberación del aire que la ciudad está volviendo a formarse a sus espaldas, temblorosos y transparentes todavía los rascacielos, como medusas del aire.

Dream City

You finally make it to the city of your dreams, but it's no longer there. Towering in its place is a mountain chain with enticing scenic views. But you didn't bring your climbing gear. No crampons, no ropes, no provisions, just a restaurant guide, a nice suit, and theater tickets. The city, in the meantime, is on the other side, and the guide offers to take you across the range by mule. And as you forge ahead slowly, thinking your spine and kidneys aren't up to this anymore, you sense in the echoes resounding in the air that the city's beginning to rise behind you again, the skyscrapers still quivery and diaphanous, like jellyfish in the air.

SUEÑOS DE NIÑOS

Si tu casa es un laberinto y en cada habitación Algo te espera,
si cobran vida los garabatos que dibujaste (tan mal) con tiza en la
pared de tu pieza, y en el living la cabeza de tu hermana ensucia
de sangre la pana del sillón verde: si hay Cosas jugando con tus
animales de plástico en la bañadera, no te preocupes, hijita, son
solamente pesadillas infantiles, ya vas a crecer, y después vas a
envejecer y después no vas a tener más sueños feos, ni te vas a
volver a despertar con angustia, no vas a tener más sueños, hijita,
ni te vas a volver a despertar.

CHILDREN'S DREAMS

If your house is a labyrinth and Something's waiting to get you in every room, if the awful chalk doodles you drew on your bedroom wall come to life, and your sister's head leaves bloody stains on the big green corduroy chair in the living room, if Things are playing with your plastic animals in the bathtub, don't worry, my baby girl, they're only childish nightmares, you'll grow up soon enough, and then you'll grow old and after that you won't have any more bad dreams, and you won't wake up scared again, you won't have any more dreams, sweetie, and you won't wake up ever again.

Convivencia imposible

El hombre pinta bien, de eso no hay duda, pero bebe mucho ajenjo, es violento, caprichoso y se hace muy difícil compartir la vida. Tomando una resolución extrema, de un sólo tajo decidido, la oreja se separa definitivamente de Van Gogh.

Impossible to Live With

The man paints well, there's no question about that, but he drinks a lot of absinthe, is violent, moody, and downright impossible to live with. Taking extreme measures, with one decisive slash, the ear takes definite leave of Van Gogh.

Van Gogh II

Suele decirse que Van Gogh se cortó la oreja para regalársela a una prostituta. Otros afirman que fue a causa de una pelea con Gauguin. Algunos científicos insisten que lo hizo porque padecía el síndrome de Ménière y lo atormentaba un acúfeno. Yo era una niñita, lo vi con mis propios ojos, y puedo asegurarle que fue para esto, para usarla de semilla, dice la anciana de Arlés, exhibiendo con orgullo el árbol cargado de frutos intrincados como caracoles, vellosos y suaves.

Van Gogh II

They say Van Gogh cut off his ear for a prostitute. Others affirm it happened in a fight with Gauguin. Some scientists insist he did it because he suffered from Ménière's Syndrome and was tormented by the ringing in his ears. I was a little girl, and I saw him with my own eyes, and I can assure you he did it for this, to use it as a seed, said the ancient woman from Arles, pointing with pride to the tree laden with spiral shaped fruit, like soft hairy snails.

Motín a bordo

Hay gente que no piensa con la cabeza: penosa situación que usted no puede permitir. Cuando los pies, el estómago, los ovarios, comienzan a tomar decisiones que le corresponden al cerebro, usted debe reprimir en forma inmediata y sin piedad ese conato de rebelión, antes de que se transforme en un motín. Si su mano derecha escandaliza, ya sabe lo que tiene que hacer. Y eso es un ejemplo, nada más. Si se eligió mencionar la mano derecha como símbolo, es justamente por su importancia, no hay por qué andarse con miramientos con el resto de su organismo: córtelos, córtelos, córtelos y arrójelos fuera de sí. Una buena cabeza firme es todo lo que se necesita, y una sencilla guillotina casera que usted mismo puede construir.

Mutiny on Board

Some people don't think with their heads, a sorry situation that you simply can't allow. When your feet, stomach, and ovaries begin to make decisions instead of your brain, you should immediately and ruthlessly put down that first stage of rebellion before it turns into mutiny. If your right hand causes you to sin, you know what you have to do. And this is just an example, nothing more. If the right hand was chosen as a symbol, it's precisely because of its importance, but there's no reason to have misgivings about your other parts: cut them off, cut them off, cut them off and throw them as far away as you can! All you need is a good head on your shoulders, and a simple home-made guillotine that you yourself can build.

La hora de las gaviotas

Es la hora de las gaviotas, los turistas se están retirando con el sol y quedan sobre la playa los detritus que señalan su paso: vasitos descartables, bolsas de plástico, latas vacías, pomos de bronceador sin tapa, hebillas rotas, palitas de juguete torcidas, papeles con restos de mostaza o mayonesa y una hermosa mujer, acostada boca arriba, que alguien se ha dejado olvidada sobre la arena, un poco triste porque sabe que pronto será borrada por las olas.

Seagull Time

The seagulls have arrived, the tourists have gone away with the last rays of sun, and on the beach lies debris, the remains of the day: disposable cups, plastic bags, empty cans, capless tubes of suntan lotion, broken barrettes, napkins smeared with mustard or mayonnaise, and a beautiful woman, lying face up, forgotten by someone who left her behind on the sand, a little sad because she knows she'll soon be washed away by the waves.

El que no tuvo infancia

Este hombre nunca fue niño, decía la gente. Y tenían razón. Producto de un embarazo prolongado, nació a los veinticinco años, en un parto trabajoso y fatal.

The Man without a Childhood

That man was never a boy, people used to say, and they were right. The result of a prolonged pregnancy, he was born at the age of twenty-five, after a difficult and fatal labor.

Poetas

Náufrago en este mundo lejano por donde no pasan ni pasarán nuestras naves, perdido en este grano de polvo apartado de todas las rutas comerciales del universo, estoy condenado a la soledad esencial de sus habitantes, incapaces de comunicarse con una herramienta menos torpe, menos opaca que el lenguaje. Yo lo utilizo para lanzar mensajes en clave que sólo los demás náufragos pueden comprender. La gente nos llama poetas.

Poets

Stranded on this distant land where spaceships don't pass nor ever will, lost on this speck of sand far from all the commercial routes of the universe, I'm condemned to share the intrinsic soltitude of its inhabitants, people incapable of communicating with a tool less unwieldy and impenetrable than language. I use it to send coded messages that only other castaways, those they call poets, can understand.

Alimentos del mar

Le gustan los calamares y los erizos, en Chile ha probado los locos y las vieyras, en Shangai aceptó encantado una medusa helada que sus anfitriones le enseñaron a comer con cucharita, ha saboreado el krill en omelettes no muy cocidos, los pepinos de mar en Indonesia, todas las variedades de algas japonesas y sin embargo algo se rebela en sus entrañas, que se niegan esta vez a retener los canapés guarnecidos (ojalá no lo hubiera sabido) con una rodajita de sirena en lata.

SEAFOOD

He likes squid and sea urchins. He's eaten mollusks and scallops in Chile, and once accepted with pleasure a frozen jellyfish in Shanghai that his hosts taught him to eat with a tiny spoon. He's savored barely-cooked krill omelettes, Indonesian sea cucumbers, and every variety of Japanese algae, and yet, something's revolting inside, refusing this time to digest those appetizers garnished (if only he hadn't known) with a slice of canned mermaid.

FORMICARIO

Qué bonitos son, ¿verdad?, sobre todo las hembras y los de
piel oscura. Lástima que vivan tan poco, pero enseguida vienen
otros a reemplazarlos. Han construido muchísimo, así, más cerca,
con esta lupa se los puede ver mejor. No todos se llevan bien
entre sí, hemos tenido problemas para evitar que se exterminen
unos a otros. Yo creo que el encierro los vuelve agresivos, si
tuviéramos más espacio donde ponerlos estarían mejor, después
de todo ya son más de seis mil millones en este pequeño mundo.

FORMICARY

Aren't they pretty, look at the females and the ones with dark
skin? Too bad they have such a short lifespan, but others come
along to replace them right away. It's incredible how much they've
built, look closer, here, you can see them better with this magni-
fying glass. Not all of them get along. We've had problems keep-
ing them from killing each other. I think being cooped up like
that makes them aggressive. If only we had more space for them,
they'd be better off, after all, now there are more than six thou-
sand millions in this tiny world.

ABOUT THE AUTHOR

Ana María Shua was born in Buenos Aires in 1951, and began her literary career at the tender age of fifteen when she published an award-winning volume of poetry *El sol y yo* (*The Sun and I*). Since then, Shua has earned a prominent place in contemporary Argentine fiction with the publication of over fifty books in nearly every literary genre: novels, short stories, sudden fiction, poetry, theater, children's fiction, books of humor and Jewish folklore, anthologies of popular myths and legends, film scripts, and essays. Her works have been translated to many languages, including English, French, German, Italian, Dutch, Swedish, and Korean, among others. She has received numerous national and international awards, and a Guggenheim Fellowship for her novel *El libro de los recuerdos* (*The Book of Memories*, 1994). Her other novels include: *Soy Paciente* (*Patient*, 1980), *Los amores de Laurita* (*Laurita's Loves*, 1984), which was made into a movie, *La muerte como efecto secundario* (*Death as a Side Effect*, 1997), which earned the Premio Club de los XIII and the Premio Ciudad de Buenos Aires, and *El peso de la tentación* (The Weight of Temptation, 2007). Her books of short stories for adults include *Viajando se conoce gente* (*You Get to Know People by Traveling*, 1988) and *Como una buena madre* (*Like a Good Mother*, 2001), among others. She has received the Diploma de Honor Konex for her short stories for adults and has won many national and international prizes for her children's fiction. The author has been invited to lecture at universities in the United States, Europe, and Latin America, and to participate in conferences. She is recognized internationally as a master of sudden fiction, and has been invited to lecture at conferences dedicated to the genre. This illustrated bilingual anthology offers a selection from the four volumes of short short stories that Shua has published to date.

About the Translator

Rhonda Dahl Buchanan is a professor of Spanish and Director of Latin American and Latino Studies at the University of Louisville. In 2000 she received the University of Louisville's Distinguished Teaching Professor Award. In 2004 she received the University of Louisville's Trustees Award and also an award to participate in a residency program at the International Banff Centre for Literary Translation in Banff, Canada. She is the author of numerous articles on contemporary Latin American writers, and the editor of a book of critical essays, *El río de los sueños: Aproximaciones críticas a la obra de Ana María Shua* (Washington, D.C.: Interamer Collection of the Organization of American States; No. 70, 2001. Available online at http://www.iacd.oas.org/Interamer/shua.htm.) She translated *Limulus: Visiones del fósil viviente* (México: Artes de México, 2004), a book by Brian Nissen and Alberto Ruy Sánchez, and is the recipient of a 2006 NEA Literature Fellowship for the translation of the Mexican writer Alberto Ruy-Sánchez's novel *Los jardines secretos de Mogador: Voces de la tierra (The Secret Gardens of Mogador: Voices of the Earth*, forthcoming, White Pine Press). Her translation, *The Entre Ríos Trilogy: Three Novels* by the Argentine writer Perla Suez was published in 2006 by the University of New Mexico Press in their Jewish Latin America Series.

About the Artist

Luci Mistratov was born Lyudmila Mistratova in Kaliningrad, Russia, and holds a Ph.D. in art education from Kaliningrad State University. She has illustrated many books of fiction and biology, and has taught art classes and won awards in numerous national and international exhibitions in Europe and the United States. Presently, she is a Scholar-in-Residence for the College of Arts and Sciences at the University of Louisville, and Director of the Kentucky Watercolor Society Gallery.

Her website is: www.mycolorworld.net.

THE WHITE PINE PRESS SECRET WEAVERS SERIES

Series General Editor: Marjorie Agosín

Dedicated to bringing the rich and varied writing
by Latin American women to the English-speaking audience.

Volume 22
A Mapmaker's Diary
Poems by Carlota Caulfield
Translated by Mary G. Berg
156 PAGES $16.00

Volume 21
Quick Fix
Sudden Fiction by Ana María Shua
Translated by Rhonda Dahl Buchanan
208 PAGES $17.00

Volume 20
Woman Without Background Music
Selected Poems of Delia Dominguez
Translated by Roberta Gordenstein and Marjorie Agosin
226 PAGES $16.00

Volume 19
With Eyes and Soul: Images of Cuba
Poems by Nancy Morejon
Photographs by Milton Rogovin
Translated by Pamela Carmell and David Frye
115 PAGES $19.00

Volume 18
I Have Forgotten Your Name
A Novel by Martha Rivera
Translated by Mary G. Berg
128 PAGES $16.00

Volume 17
Open Your Eyes and Soar
Cuban Women Writing Now
Edited by Mary G. Berg
192 PAGES $16.00

Volume 16
A Woman in Her Garden
Selected Poems of Dulce María Loynaz
Translated by Judith Kerman
176 PAGES $16.00

Volume 15
Gabriela Mistral: Recados on Women
Translated by Jacqueline C. Nanfito
224 PAGES $16.00

Volume 14
River of Sorrows
A Novel by Libertad Demitropulos
Translated by Mary G. Berg
160 PAGES $14.00

Volume 13
A Secret Weavers Anthology:
Selections from the White Pine Press Secret Weavers Series
232 PAGES $14.00

Volume 12
Ximena at the Crossroads
A novel by Laura Riesco
Translated by Mary G. Berg
Out of Print

Volume 11
A Necklace of Words
Short Fiction by Mexican Women
152 PAGES $14.00

Volume 10
≥
A Novel by Rosario Aguilar
Translated by Edward Waters Hood
Out of Print

Volume 9
What is Secret
Stories by Chilean Women
304 PAGES $17.00

Volume 8
Happy Days, Uncle Sergio
A Novel by Magali García Ramis
Translated by Carmen C. Esteves
OUT OF PRINT

Volume 7
These Are Not Sweet Girls
Poetry by Latin American Women
368 PAGES $20.00

Volume 6
Pleasure in the Word
Erotic Fiction by Latin American Women
Ed. by Margarite Fernández Olmos & Lizabeth Paravisini-Gebert
240 PAGES $19.95 CLOTH

Volume 5
A Gabriela Mistrel Reader
Translated by Maria Giacchetti
232 PAGES $15.00

Volume 3
Landscapes of a New Land
Short Fiction by Latin American Women
194 PAGES $12.00

Volume 1
Alfonsina Storni: Selected Poems
Edited by Marion Freeman
72 PAGES $8.00 PAPER